WORDS AND SYMBC

Core Concepts in Therapy

Series editor: Michael Jacobs

Over the last ten years a significant shift has taken place in the relations between representatives of different schools of therapy. Instead of the competitive and often hostile reactions we once expected from each other, therapists from different points of the spectrum of approaches are much more interested in where they overlap and where they differ. There is a new sense of openness to cross-orientation learning.

The Core Concepts in Therapy series compares and contrasts the use of similar terms across a range of therapeutic models, and seeks to identify where different terms appear to denote similar concepts. Each book is authored by two therapists, each one from a distinctly different orientation; and where possible each one from a different continent, so that an international dimension becomes a feature of this network of ideas.

Each of these short volumes examines a key concept in psychological therapy, setting out comparative positions in a spirit of free and critical enquiry, but without the need to prove one model superior to another. The books are fully referenced and point beyond themselves to the wider literature on each topic.

Forthcoming and published titles:

Paul Brinich and Christopher Shelley: *The Self and Personality Structure*
Dilys Davies and Dinesh Bhugra: *Models of Psychopathology*
David Edwards and Michael Jacobs: *Conscious and Unconscious*
Dawn Freshwater and Chris Robertson: *Emotions and Needs*
Jan Grant and Jim Crawley: *Transference and Projection*
Richard J. Hazler and Nick Barwick: *The Therapeutic Environment*
John Davy and Malcolm Cross: *Barriers, Defences and Resistance*
John Rowan and Michael Jacobs: *The Therapist's Use of Self*
Lynn Seiser and Colin Wastell: *Interventions and Techniques*
Gabrielle Syme and Jennifer Elton Wilson: *Objectives and Outcomes*
Val Simanowitz and Peter Pearce: *Personality Development*
Nick Totton and Michael Jacobs: *Character and Personality Types*
Kenneth C. Wallis and James L. Poulton: *Internalization*

WORDS AND SYMBOLS: LANGUAGE AND COMMUNICATION IN THERAPY

Nicola Barden

and

Tina Williams

 Open University Press

Open University Press
McGraw-Hill Education
McGraw-Hill House
Shoppenhangers Road
Maidenhead
Berkshire
England
SL6 2QL

email: enquiries@openup.co.uk
world wide web: www.openup.co.uk

and Two Penn Plaza, New York, NY 10121-2289, USA

First published 2007

A catalogue record of this book is available from the British Library

ISBN-10: 0 335 21361 8 (pb)   0 335 21362 6 (hb)
ISBN-13: 978 0 335 21361 0 (pb)   978 0 335 21362 7 (hb)

Library of Congress Cataloguing-in-Publication Data
CIP data applied for

Typeset by RefineCatch Limited, Bungay, Suffolk
Printed in the UK by Bell & Bain Ltd, Glasgow

The **McGraw·Hill** Companies

Contents

Series editor's foreword

A major aspect of intellectual and cultural life in the twentieth century has been the study of psychology – present of course for many centuries in practical form and expression in the wisdom and insight to be found in spirituality, in literature and in the dramatic arts, as well as in arts of healing and guidance, both in the East and West. In parallel with the deepening interest in the inner processes of character and relationships in the novel and theatre in the nineteenth century, psychiatry reformulated its understanding of the human mind, and encouraged, in those brave enough to challenge the myths of mental illness, new methods of exploration of psychological processes.

The twentieth century witnessed, especially in its latter half, an explosion of interest both in theories about personality, psychological development, cognition and behaviour, as well as in the practice of therapy, or perhaps more accurately, the therapies. It also saw, as is not uncommon in any intellectual discipline, battles between theories and therapists of different persuasions, particularly between psychoanalysis and behavioural psychology, and each in turn with humanistic and transpersonal therapies, and also within the major schools themselves. If such arguments are not surprising, and indeed objectively can be seen as healthy – potentially promoting greater precision in research, alternative approaches to apparently intractable problems, and deeper understanding of the wellsprings of human thought, emotion and behaviour – it is nonetheless disturbing that for many decades there was such a degree of sniping and entrenchment of positions from therapists who should have been able to look more closely at their own responses and rivalries. It is as if diplomats had ignored their skills and knowledge and resorted in their dealings with each other to gun slinging.

The psychotherapeutic enterprise has also been an international one. There were a large number of centres of innovation, even at the beginning – Paris, Moscow, Vienna, Berlin, Zurich, London, Boston USA, and soon Edinburgh, Rome, New York, Chicago and California saw the development of different theories and therapeutic practice. Geographical location has added to the richness of the discipline, particularly identifying cultural and social differences, and widening the psychological debate to include, at least in some instances, sociological and political dimensions.

The question has to be asked, given the separate developments due to location, research interests, personal differences, and splits between and within traditions, whether what has sometimes been called 'psycho-babble' is indeed a welter of different languages describing the same phenomena through the particular jargon and theorizing of the various psychotherapeutic schools. Or are there genuine differences, which may lead sometimes to the conclusion that one school has got it right, while another has therefore got it wrong, or that there are 'horses for courses', or, according to the Dodo principle, that 'all shall have prizes'?

The latter part of the twentieth century saw some rapprochement between the different approaches to the theory and practice of psychotherapy (and counselling), often due to the external pressures towards organizing the profession responsibly and to the high standards demanded of it by health care, by the public and by the state. It is out of this budding rapprochement that there came the motivation for this series, in which a number of key concepts that lie at the heart of the psychotherapies can be compared and contrasted across the board. Some of the terms used in different traditions may prove to represent identical concepts; others may look similar, but in fact highlight quite different emphases, which may or may not prove useful to those who practice from a different perspective; other terms, apparently identical, may prove to mean something completely different in two or more schools of psychotherapy.

In order to carry out this project it seemed essential that as many of the psychotherapeutic traditions as possible should be represented in the authorship of the series, and to promote both this, and the spirit of dialogue between traditions, it seemed also desirable that there should be two authors for each book, each one representing, where practicable, different orientations. It was important that the series should be truly international in its approach and therefore in its authorship, and that miracle of late twentieth-century technology – the Internet – proved to be a productive means of finding authors, as well as a remarkably efficient method of communicating, in the cases of some pairs of authors, half-way across the world.

This series therefore represents, in a new millennium, an extremely exciting development, one that as series editor I have found more and more enthralling as I have eavesdropped on the drafts shuttling back and forth between authors. Here, for the first time, the reader will find all the major concepts of all the principal schools of psychotherapy and counselling (and not a few minor ones) drawn together so that they may be compared, contrasted, and (it is my hope) above all used – used for the ongoing debate between orientations, but more importantly still, used for the benefit of clients and patients who are not at all interested in partisan positions, but in what works, or in what throws light upon their search for healing and understanding.

Michael Jacobs

At the Time

Some haunt because of a wrong they did
Or one done them and either way
The dead trail with the living still
Beyond amends. But all you did

Was keep your distance at the time,
Being shy perhaps, and only watched
And never came over, hoping perhaps
I'd notice and I'd be the one who'd cross

And free the talk, for the only gap
Between us then was the living years.
I should have asked more of you at the time
But I kept my distance and never did.

Now you trail me along the river as though
Upstream or down there might be a place,
Beyond being shy, to cross but each
Must always keep his distance now,

Make do with his monologue either side
Like the whispering reeds and the burden still
Is that I should have come over for
Your conversation at the time.

(Constantine 2004)

Prologue – or before the word

Nicola Barden

When Michael Jacobs, the series editor, first asked for indications of interest in co-authoring *Words and Symbols* I immediately wanted to respond, but had no time to offer at that point, and was not sure either that I had the ability. I was very pleased when the opportunity became available again a couple of years later, and perhaps rather more confident, thinking it was too good an opportunity to pass up again.

The project had run into some difficulties as the previous authors had been unable to fulfil their commitments. Co-authoring is extremely important in this series as each book needs to provide a broad perspective across theoretical orientations on the specific concept under consideration. Although I have some background in person-centred work, my training and therapeutic mindset is clearly analytic, and I knew I was not competent to give voice to the other orientations except at a very basic level. It was in part the Jungian emphasis in my training that piqued my interest in the title of the book: words and symbols were of great importance to Jung, who was fascinated by the meaning of symbols and the use of imagination, myth and story in relation to the unconscious. So I was grateful to be paired with a colleague whose grasp of the issues was clear to see, and felt the loss badly when he had to withdraw for completely understandable personal reasons.

I put out feelers for another co-author. Tina responded to an e-mail circular, and we met for an exploratory session in the middle of a conference that I was attending near her home. I recall being delighted by her enthusiasm and interest in the project. My experience of writing to date is that it has its ups and its downs, and the best safeguard against burnout is to have some passion for the subject. So, although we had never worked together, did not know each other and lived a couple of hundred miles apart, we agreed at that point to undertake the project together. I hoped the physical distance could be overcome through e-mail, and that the shared interest in the topic would somehow see us through any difficulties. Looking for a co-author is not unlike looking for a therapist in that you do not really know what he or she will be like until you have started, no matter how thoroughly you do the research. Once you have established basic competence the relationship is as good a predictor of outcome as anything else.

Books are generally written around all of the other commitments in life, and life is unpredictable. During the course of the two years of writing this book Tina and I between us changed jobs, took on other major commitments and negotiated changing family circumstances. Two years is not long to write a book, and I was responsible for the wild enthusiasm that anticipated a 12-month timescale. This left us subsequently requiring large quantities of patience from our families and partners, our editor, our publishers and each other. The e-mail communication was fraught. Our computers would not 'talk' to each other; I lost track of or confused which were the latest versions of chapters because of working on home and work computers simultaneously. We did manage to meet a couple more times and this felt good to do, but the meetings were always squeezed between other activities and basically functional. Communication took place through the medium of the book itself for me – reading each other's chapters, slowly getting a feel for each other's styles and preferences and *how* we both wrote, as well as what we wanted to say. Because Tina came into a pre-existing book the style was already set, and this was challenging for her as her natural preference is to write in the first person. I have always written in the third person, and that feels natural to me. We have reflected a little since as to whether, for us, this matches our different theoretical orientations. While I would disagree with Tina's suggestion in the epilogue that a humanistic therapist moves forward towards relationship while the psychoanalytic therapist moves away from it, there is something about how the relationship is approached that may be unique to each. Psychotherapy is a deeply process-oriented activity and I am rather a task-focused individual. What sustains me as a therapist is the pleasure of a good connection made between myself and the client, usually through an accurate and shared understanding of the material at a meaningful level. At this moment process and task come together. It was too easy in the task of co-authoring for me to pay insufficient attention to process and to assume we would be held together by what we were both *doing*, and there certainly was an irony that rewarded reflection when our e-mails to each other were returned as undeliverable!

The subject of the book has proved even more interesting to me than I had anticipated. The pleasure of writing with someone from a different theoretical orientation lay in encountering and negotiating difference, and also simply in learning a great deal more about humanistic approaches. I have been grateful to Tina for checking that I was along the right lines when attempting to write outside my direct experience. This meant I could risk putting into words things that I could not have said on my personal authority alone.

Others I would like to thank include Michael Jacobs, the series editor, for sound and steady guidance; David Constantine and Bloodaxe Books for kind permission to include his poem 'At the Time'; my friends and colleagues, for their generous interest and support; and most especially my partner, Caroline, for being such a delight through it all.

Tina Williams

'Co-author needed'. Not being someone to turn down an opportunity I responded immediately. No problem, I naively thought, I can do that. This is what can happen when you get empowered by personal therapy. I can still feel the sense of euphoria when Nicola agreed to my being involved. Thus began a two-year-plus marathon.

What I had not appreciated, not having attempted anything of this size before, was the huge time commitment involved. Against a backdrop of all the other normal events in the course of everyday family life, in every spare moment, on the weekends, when I should have been doing something else at work, I was either reading or researching for, writing or indeed thinking about writing, The Book (as it has come to be known by my very long-suffering family). In fact it feels as though this project has become so much a part of my life that I will grieve its passing into the other world of completed books in the public domain.

The physical distance between myself and Nicola meant that, with the exception of the occasional phone call and three short face-to-face meetings, we had to rely almost entirely on e-mail communication.

Everybody knows how wonderful computer technology is but I certainly had not appreciated the horrendous confusion it can lead to when it does not work. E-mails not delivered, files that refused to open or to be amended, amendments that disappeared: these were just a few of our problems. In the final stages two of the computers we used refused to accept e-mails from each other. All of this made our communication very complicated at times. An old friend of mine would have referred to this as the 'animate cursedness of inanimate objects', and I think that there was undoubtedly a connection between animate user and the inanimate object. One connection between me and the computer problems that we had might have been the insidious nature of procrastination and the anxiety it creates as deadlines creep closer. Having recently worked at a university I am fully aware of how effective a barrier this can be to being able to finish anything and how many seemingly unrelated obstacles can crop up to prevent the final piece of work being ready on time. There was also an element of committing myself to paper. Once I had pressed the 'send' button that was it: whatever I had written was then out there to be judged. Words, whether written or spoken, are a reflection of ourselves, a part of our personality that we present to the world. As I have become more and more aware in writing the book, this everyday aspect of communicating is both friend and foe to our true self. Writing has helped me to recognize the importance for the therapeutic relationship of acknowledging these two faces of both our own and our clients' words.

I have pondered over what attracted me to the idea of being involved in writing this book. I have never been someone who has felt any great desire to share my opinions or thoughts or indeed my feelings with others, strangely enough for someone who has chosen to be a therapist, so what on earth was in it for me? As with anything connected with therapy, when I feel brave enough to be totally honest about the attraction of this project and to take time to really reflect on my involvement, I realize that actually it is much more about a personal journey – in one sense any benefit that the reader may get is incidental to that.

I have been very aware, during the process of being involved with the book, of the history of the project before I joined it. Nicola and I are the third combination to attempt it. There were no doubt good reasons why the other potential authors dropped out, but it seems ironic that a book on words and symbols has itself proved so difficult to write. Sometimes too close an examination of what we automatically do, making us conscious of things we may not have previously thought about, can bring us to a halt. It is like driving. Years of smoothly coordinated actions can suddenly become impossible when you start to think through exactly what it is you are required to do at any given moment. I have at times been left with a definite sense of how possible it is to disappear into an abyss of questions. Nevertheless, asking those questions, as I indicate in the epilogue, has proved valuable to my work as a therapist.

I wish to thank my family, Steve, Sam and Grace, for being there and continuing to put up with me, the University of Leicester for providing me with many resources, and the Laura Centre for giving me renewed inspiration.

C H A P T E R   1

Learning language: historical and contemporary perspectives

Nicola Barden and Tina Williams

Language has been a subject of study for around 3000 years, although humans have been talking to each other in all likelihood since *homo sapiens* evolved in Africa 200,000 years ago. Humans remain the only species with the mental and physical capacity to transform thoughts into words, to think in words, to create and communicate with the symbolic notation of experience that is called language. Words are commonly used without awareness of their presence, much as breath is drawn without awareness of the task of breathing or of the surrounding air. Psychotherapy by contrast pays detailed attention to what is said, how and by whom. In most modalities it is an activity almost entirely conducted through the medium of language, and examination of that language is an integral part of therapeutic work. Putting experience into words is viewed as therapeutic in itself as it both names and communicates what may have been hidden and without form, bringing the self back into relationship with the environment, with others, with itself. Given that therapy places such store on language, it is useful to know a little more about it. Most therapists will know little about the acquisition of language or its place in mental processes. Children are assumed to pick language up from their parents; therapy has concentrated on what happens next.

So what exactly is meant by language? And how has language come to play such an important part in communication between people? This chapter starts by looking at the phenomenon of language itself. A historical and contemporary review sets the scene for the more clinical chapters that follow.

A brief history of the study of language

Learning a 'mother tongue' does not happen through formal teaching. It is common to be fluent in a language without having to consider how it is put together or what stops it falling apart. It just *is*. Yet as therapy takes apart the meaning of words spoken in the consulting room, it could benefit from a greater curiosity about the way words are formed, the choices available in the construction of speech, the processes through which a child acquires speech and how language manages its continuous existence despite all the pressures upon it for change. Indeed, linguists estimate that over the course of 10,000 years a language changes so completely that the original one has ceased to exist and a new one has taken its place, but the journey from the one to the other remains traceable.

Over 6000 languages are spoken in the world today. Complex languages have been associated with civilized, industrialized society, and many early linguistic explorers anticipated 'primitive' forms of language, contiguous with the pervasive and colonial concept of 'primitive' tribes that were somehow less 'civilized' than Western Europe or North America. Therapeutic thought was not exempt from this – Carl Jung, a keen student of other cultures as he formulated his idea of the collective unconscious, which he saw as a repository of the collected experiences of humankind enshrined in the archetypes common to us all, looked positively towards 'primitive' tribes in Africa. He felt they were still able to contain and demonstrate some of the more unconscious aspects of humanity through rituals and beliefs that Jung valued as true and essential while, by this very valuing, construing them as undeveloped. 'Primitive' languages were expected to share largely the level of a toddler's acquisition of language – nouns strung together with a few connecting phrases. A more modern understanding of languages is one that insists that even toddlers are using a complex system of grammar, one appropriate to the level of language acquisition they have at the time, but entire in itself rather than an incomplete imitation of adult speech (McNeill 1966).

This was demonstrated in a commercial expedition in New Guinea led by Michael Leahy in 1930. At that time the country's population included missionaries, prospectors and farmers, who had all settled in the coastal lowlands, leaving an unvisited mountain range running down the middle of the island which was assumed to be uninhabited. What Leahy discovered when he ascended the hills in search of gold was a grassy and very inhabited plateau at the top, with people who 'jabbered' constantly when he appeared and pointed at all that was new to them in this meeting, not least the white man himself (Pinker 1994: 26). In fact the 'jabbering' was a complex language – one of 800 discovered to be spoken on the plateau – with nothing primitive about it, in a place so cut off that if there was an association between the development of language and connectedness with the outside world it could not reasonably have been expected to be visible here. Pinker reflects that this universality of language – no community has ever been 'discovered' that did not have a complex language – is 'the first reason to suspect that language is not just any cultural invention but the product of a special human instinct' (p. 26).

So far from language developing from crude beginnings, it would seem that even isolated languages developed with sophistication and with a clear set of rules. The first written record of the rules underlying language was made by Indian grammarian Panini who wrote the *Astadhayayi* in the fifth century BC, bringing together even earlier studies on the structure of language. Panini's concept was that words came together through the joining of a number of component parts, and that rules were then applied to words to enable them to form recognizable sentences. This simple but encompassing framework has not been bettered, and indeed forms the foundation of much modern thinking on language, including that of Noam Chomsky, possibly the most influential linguistic scholar of the twentieth century.

In the fourth century BC Greek language theories were formed that are still the basis for European grammar today, with Aristotle defining subject and predicate, and over the next couple of centuries Dyscolus and Thrax defining nouns, verbs, articles, pronouns, prepositions, conjunctions, adverbs and participles. English lessons today remain based on these 2000-year-old principles.

Linguists have struggled with the question of whether all languages evolved from one original language, changing over time in the course of migration and war. From the late eighteenth century similarities between certain languages were sufficiently remarked on to posit the existence of a common 'Proto-Indo-European', or PIE, ancestor, which eventually gave birth to languages as different as Portuguese, Bengali, Lithuanian and English. This can be traced back to communities living 6000 years ago somewhere in Eurasia, moving through Scandinavia where the language became 'Proto-Germanic' into northern Europe and eventually into Britain. PIE itself may have been produced by even more ancestral languages, with the possibility of one far-away head of the linguistic family tree, but tracing this has so far been inconclusive, and the fact that languages change so much over time contributes to the difficulty (Trask and Mayblin 2000).

Considering the ancestry of language begs the question of whether it came all at once in a kind of linguistic 'big bang' (Bickerton 1981), or whether, as Pinker suggests, language is an evolutionary, instinctual process, hard wired into the brain through years of natural selection. Bickerton cites the absence of crude, simplistic languages among any of those discovered to date as evidence in the same way that anti-evolutionists have looked for the 'missing link' to gainsay Darwinism. Pinker (1994) uses the information to support the hypotheses that the complexity of language must be an evolutionary process, in the same way that the development of an eyeball relied on countless generations seeing better and therefore surviving better until eyeballs just became part of the genetic picture. In doing this he also argued that the instinctive development of language only occurred in humans. The structure of the mouth, with the vocal chords dropping after infancy to allow a resonant cavity in the back of the throat, is unique to humans. Primates use the subcortical part of their brain when they vocalize – the same part that humans use when crying, laughing, moaning, or making other vocalizations that are not language. Language, as opposed to sound, is controlled by the cerebral cortex, and is a voluntary, human act. Animals in this view can communicate, but they cannot talk.

Learning language

Language is such a taken-for-granted part of adult life that it can be hard to appreciate the complexity involved in learning it. But language acquisition poses fundamental questions as to what it is to be human. Do children learn to talk through observation, repetition and reward, as behaviourists like Skinner (1957) believed, following the behavioural style of Pavlov? In this view thought and speech are inseparable: children can think when they can talk (Slobin 1971). Or does cognitive development precede speech, as Piaget concluded (Beard 1969), with language assisting the process but not causing it?

In a sense, Skinner was talking about speech while Piaget was talking about language. Sounds themselves do not constitute language, although they facilitate it. Attempts to construe everyday words as onomatopoeic fail in the translation from one language to another. The words chosen to represent things are arbitrarily conceived. Saussure (1916/1959), a Swiss linguist working in the late nineteenth and early twentieth centuries, pointed out that meaning was contained not in the link between the thing and its name, but in a more subtle link between a concept and a sound pattern. What lies between the concept and the sound pattern is the hearer, and thus Saussure paved the way for thinking about the significance of inter-pretation, or the meaning given by the listener to what they are hearing. This was the beginning of the 'structuralist' approach to lan-guage, in which the meaning of a word was understood through its relationship to other words, the whole sentence structure. The small-est structures are phonemes, or single phonetic sounds. These join to make words, and words join according to certain rules to make sen-tences. Meaning is derived by understanding the relationship of all of these component parts to each other; language is essentially made up of an orderly system of orderly systems. Saussure's thinking was built upon by Jakobson (Trask and Mayblin 2000) who took it into the field of semiotics, or the study of signs and symbols in language. Language was not the only purveyor of meaning; signs or symbols were to be found in other dimensions, and meaning could be construed from them. This theory had a particular influence in France, and can be seen in the work of Lacan, Foucault and Derrida.

For children to learn languages, then, they must learn both the words that make up speech, and the rules by which these words are put together. For this to happen the rules must be clear, and anom-alies must be consistent. Chomsky (1957) formed a comprehensive system that he called 'generative grammar', which gave boundaries to the English language that aimed to encompass everything it could and could not do. In the end this was extremely difficult to achieve, but in the course of the work Chomsky developed the powerful theory that rules of grammar are inbuilt, that people are born with the equivalent of a linguistic template which then interacts with the actual experience of language as it is met in the world. This was one of the only ways of explaining the ability demonstrated by children in grasping extremely complex language structures with such rapidity and success. Pinker (1994) took Chomsky's work a stage further and posited the existence of a language instinct, in the Darwinian sense of an adaptive genetic language trait in humans. His foremost argument for this is based on observations of children learning to talk: 'complex language is universal because *children actually reinvent it*, generation after generation – not because they are taught, not because they are generally smart, not because it is helpful to them, but because they just can't help it' (p. 32).

As examples he cites the transformation in one generation of 'pidgin' – a makeshift language with very basic vocabulary and gram-mar made from two or more speech communities, where neither

group spoke the other's language – into 'creole'. Creole is a sophisti-
cated language deriving from pidgin, as the children of the pidgin
speakers naturally started to apply to it their inbuilt knowledge of the
structure of language. Another example comes from the observation
of deaf children who, when taught rudimentary signing from hearing
parents, immediately improve on it, grasping what it is that the parents are trying to achieve. Trask and Mayblin (2000) cite deaf children
in Nicaragua who, freed from institutions after the 1979 revolution,
quickly constructed among themselves a grammatically coherent sign
language that became the base for modern Nicaraguan sign language.
In the most adverse conditions, and without being taught, children
will create a language. Not a Stone Age one, but one with words and
rules and meaning. It is, according to Pinker, all genes and brain.

Children's interest in communication can be noticed from birth.
Careful infant observation shows their awareness of sounds and sen-
sations, their ability to grasp patterns and to see gaps in patterns, their
searching exploration of the world as they make sense of it. Infants
can discriminate between similar sounds at 1 month old, for example
'pa' and 'ba'. By 2 months this extends to two syllables, for example
'bada' and 'baga' (Bee 1994). At 6 months they will make sense of
the sound no matter who says it, whereas previously it was easier
within familiar relationships. Producing sounds takes longer than
recognizing them. Babies explore their own sound-making capacities
at 5 months, a while after the larynx has descended, allowing the
tongue to move and produce a wide range of sounds. At 7 months
they are babbling. Deaf children also go through the babbling stage
(Bee 1994; Fry 1966), using sign language rather than sound if that is
how their parents have communicated with them. Babbling plays
with and practices the complex range of sounds the infant can make
until they have an element of mastery, and can begin to learn words,
generally after the first birthday. Use of single words initially carries
complex meanings as there is not yet a capacity for precision: 'juice'
can mean 'that's juice', 'give me some juice', 'I want the juice *now*'. By
18 months they are learning new words at the rate of one every two
hours, and soon start to pair them up. By 3 years old grammar is well
under way. Pinker (1994) demonstrates the rapidity of this development with the example of 'Adam', who at 2 years and 3 months could
say 'A bunny-rabbit walk'; at 2 years and 10 months 'You don't have
paper'; and by 3 years and 2 months, 'When it's got a flat tire it needs
to go to the station' (p. 270). A school-age child in America has an
average vocabulary of 13,000 words; a high-school graduate 60,000
(Pinker 1999). The rate of memory learning at a young age is phe-

nomenal. By 3 and a half years, language acquisition is complete (McNeill 1966) in the sense that the child both understands and manipulates the basic rules that apply to sentence construction.

Do children learn all this from observing and listening to other adults talk to or teach them? While the facilitative role of being in communication with others is not in question, Pinker's examples of an inbuilt instinct are compelling.

Piaget posited two essential processes underlying learning: adaptation to the environment and organization of experience (Beard 1969). He saw infants as inhabiting a primarily sensori-motor world, with responses being adaptive and survival based. Reflex reactions are what the infant brings into the world – sucking when placed in contact with a nipple, grasping the adult finger placed in the palm. From the interaction of reflex with environment a repertoire of responses is built up to be repeated in similar situations, or adapted in unfamiliar ones. Through play these repetitions and adaptations are assimilated to become a part of the internal map, or cognitive schema, of the infant's world. By 18 months Piaget's infant is able to begin turning cognitions into representations, that is, to represent the world internally through language and symbols. Piaget does not see language as necessary for representation to begin with, but it becomes more important later, as language replaces actions and enables feelings and desires to be held in the mind and communicated through words, without the need for direct actions. The object is represented internally. In this view language is learned by experience and reflects rather than determines the cognitive development of the child; there is no innate tendency to develop language in a particular way.

Piaget to a degree followed a tradition existing since St Augustine, that children learn language by hearing it spoken and by imitating what they hear, using trial and error and learning from correction. Yet close observation of how adults talk to children, and how children go about constructing their conversations, puts this generally accepted view into doubt. For example, children do learn huge numbers of words by rote, usually starting with nouns – dog, cat, mummy, blanky, and so on – frequently repeated by parents. Similarly they learn verbs – 'go', 'give', 'buy'. The most commonly used, and therefore first learned, verbs are irregular, and have to be memorized as they do not obey consistent rules – the past tense is 'went', 'gave', 'bought'. Regular verbs when acquired then lead to some confusion. The child sees a pattern to 'wanted', 'sorted', 'chopped', and imposes this pattern on the memorized irregular verbs, making 'goed', 'gived', 'buyed'. As adults will never have taught the child these incorrect constructions, the process can be seen as evidence of the child's own mental work in understanding language, which is going on independently of the adult's teaching. Though children rely on adults to correct them, they seem to learn not by imitating the corrections but by gradually learning the rules implied by the corrections, and memorizing the words that they do not apply to, until they can apply them themselves. McNeill (1966) gives an example of this in terms of the use of negatives, from a 1964 study by Ervin, recording a conversation between mother and child:

> *Child*: Nobody don't like me.
> *Mother*: No, say 'nobody likes me'.
> *Child*: Nobody don't like me.
> Eight repetitions of this exact sequence then follow. Then:
> *Mother*: No, now listen carefully; say *'nobody likes me'*.
> *Child*: Oh! Nobody don't like*s* me.
>
> (p. 69)

Slobin emphasizes children's responsiveness to patterns. Even as babies they can identify changes to patterns. Having observed patterns they can reproduce them, extend the implied rule to new situations, and spot deviations. This makes them natural linguists as they grasp a rule of sentence construction, extend this to a new situation and then make improvements to it in the light of experience. This illustrates the inbuilt tendency to create language claimed by Chomsky and Pinker. Opponents of the instinctual view emphasize the political and philosophical influences on the development of language, and the differences between languages and even within the same language, as indicative of the unlikelihood of some sort of universal language code. The conflict, however, often comes down to the level of detail being ascribed to the theory. Unlike Chomsky, Pinker sees the language instinct applying purely on a meta-level, not dissimilar from the way in which Jung considered the application of archetypal theory to the collective unconscious. Just as psychological archetypes are overarching concepts describing universal human themes, so 'Universal Grammar is like an archetypal body plan found across vast numbers of animals in a phylum' (Pinker 1994: 238). As the same parts of a skeleton are traceable in all vertebrates, albeit in very different forms, so common traits are visible across all the world's languages. Pinker as an evolutionist finds support in Darwin, who wrote, 'The formation of different languages and of distinct species, and the proofs that both have been developed through a gradual process, are curiously parallel . . . We find in distinct languages striking homologies due to community of descent, and analogies due to a similar process of formation' (Pinker 1994: 241).

Children hear language spoken, whether verbally or through signing, and language development follows similar stages whether the individual is fully hearing, hearing impaired or deaf. What they hear is assessed against 'formal and substantive universals' (McNeill 1966: 38), and a hypothesis is formed to be tested out in speech and modified as necessary. Having these universals limits the amount of testing and modification that is required and makes the whole project of language acquisition feasible, while being spoken to helps a child see the available options within the universals more quickly than if they had to work alone. New words and sentence constructions are taken up like toys and played with to increase overall skill and mastery.

Mind, body and language

Neuroscience as a distinct field of study has developed since the 1950s and 1960s, merging the traditional fields of biological studies – neuroanatomy, neurochemistry, neurophysiology and physiological psychology. It is the study of the structure, function, development, chemistry, pharmacology and pathology of the central nervous system. Developments in neuroscience have now begun to provide an understanding of how the brain grows and develops to allow a language to be learnt. As a result a fascinating correlation between the emotional, verbal and physical development of the growing infant is becoming clearer.

The world of neuroscience has had a huge impact on the understanding of language development, helping to build up a picture of the specific location within the brain of the various components that allow language to be used. This, however, is not straightforward and it seems that the more that is known the more complex it becomes.

Language involves a combination of the motor skills that permit the use of tongue and mouth to form words, and the cognition that enables an understanding of the rules of language and indeed the capacity to use them. Research points to these functions being predominantly situated in the left brain hemisphere (Ronnberg et al. 2002). An area of the brain called Broca's area, close to the motor control for the mouth, is responsible for the delicate control needed to form words and to speak them in an understandable way.

The cognitive function of the brain associated with language com-prehension known as Wernicke's area has been found in a site associ-ated with hearing, the auditory cortex (Camarata and Yoder 2002), again in the left hemisphere. This suggests that language has more connection with auditory than visual capacities, tested by what are known as 'split brain experiments'. In medical conditions where sep-arating the brain has been necessary so that the connection between the left and right hemisphere is broken (for example in some forms of epilepsy treatment) experiments show that visual recognition takes place in the right half of the brain while the ability to correctly name an object and to verbalize that name takes place in the left hemi-sphere. This is also demonstrated by those who suffer aphasia as a result of brain damage, who can correctly recognize an object but are unable to verbalize it, perhaps recognizing 'a tin opener' but saying 'a book'.

As children grow physically so their brains develop. Specifically, research has shown that as the child grows their brain synapses grow (Brierly and Barlow 1994). The synapses provide links between neurons or nerve cells and it is these that are crucial to the processes of thought and perception, and are a fundamental part of the healthy development of the child. The development of the brain peaks at between 9 months and 2 years, with metabolic activity in the brain reaching adult levels by 9–10 months and peaking around 4 years. Neuroscientist Alan Schore (2001) relates this understanding to the work of Daniel Stern, a developmentalist, and suggests that the place of language as part of the child's world, and their way of relating to it, is made possible because the right hemisphere begins a growth spurt around the same time which allows it to interact with the left hemi-sphere which is also maturing and developing. The study within neuroscience of the parts of the brain that are responsible for lan-guage acquisition means that there is now a greater understanding of how these interrelate with the capacity for affect and creativity as well as other cognitive abilities.

Schore (1994) refers to the work of Buck that language is not solely a cognitive product: 'strong motivational and emotional forces invigorate the learning of language and infuse its application with intensity and energy' (p. 266). Language is not just a cognitive skill but also a creative skill that involves imagination and emotions. This notion of human development and use of language as a holistic reflection of the ability to feel and think links symbol formation with the capacity to recognize and tolerate absence from the other and with creativity and imagination. It is of crucial importance in understanding the role of verbal communication in therapy. It is a concept that will be returned to in later chapters.

Neuroscience certainly facilitates recognition of these links. While seeing the left hemisphere of the brain as largely responsible for the acquisition of language, it is clear that as well as other non-verbal events, 'verbal spontaneous emotional communications' are outputs of the right brain attachment system (Schore 2001: 44). The left hemisphere is responsible for most linguistic tasks but the right hemisphere is the origin of broader communication. As the toddler grows into the older child interaction with peers relies on the right hemispheric ability to read facial expressions and tones of voice in order to have emotional attunement with others and to respond appropriately. The developing child can use language in a way that fits the pattern that the adult world surrounding the child expects. The location of language within the brain helps the understanding of how language is used. There is a growing body of evidence that the development of the capacity to use language is intrinsically connected with emotional development.

Language and the sense of self

Stern's (2000) groundbreaking work explores the way in which growing infants develop their relationship not only with the world around them but also with themselves. This provides them with a new social life, a sense of self that opens up as their linguistic ability grows, preparing a way for them to organize their perspective of all interpersonal events. This is the 'verbal stage' of Stern's infant development, the final of four stages: the sense of an emergent self, the sense of a core self, the sense of a subjective self and the sense of a verbal self.

The first of these, the emergent self, starting at around 2 months, is the process that the child goes through in recognizing that they are the person that all the different experiences they encounter are happening to. Any experience the child has, any sensation, action, perception, thought or feeling, is recognized as causing a reaction that defines the child as involved in the experience, having a 'self' which is making sense of experience. Stern (2000: xvii) describes this as 'experiencing being alive while encountering the world'.

The next phase, the core sense of self, Stern divides into 'self versus other' and 'self with other', beginning at around 3 months. This is the period during which the child starts to experience being in relation to but also being distinct from the other. Stern lists different aspects of this experience for the child as self-agency: control over actions; self-coherence: a sense of being a whole person with boundaries; self-history: a belief in a past that gives reassurance of continuity into the future; and self-affectivity: an expansion of the emergent self in experiencing affect in response to events.

This sets the scene for the next stage in development as the child starts to use words and develops a verbal sense of self during their second year of life. Through this process the sense of self and the sense of other change. A distinction emerges for the infant between their own personal knowledge of the world and that of the other. The possibility of a new way of sharing these differences emerges with the infant's growing capacity to use language. Stern describes the twofold task of this stage of development as the ability to share personal experiences and to share being with others. The infant learns to share meaning, to be understood and to understand others.

Stern (2000) refers to the 'slippage' that can occur between the personal world knowledge of the child and 'official' or 'socialized' knowledge that is encoded in language. This occurs because language is better at describing the various types of emotional states – angry, happy, scared, anxious – than the dimensional features of the affect – how angry, how happy. So language is geared up for categorical descriptions rather than the nuances of representing the gradient of the affective state. Slippage also occurs between experience and words. Language cannot precisely describe the experience of emotional connection to someone without a word having to be exchanged. An experience cannot be retold without being changed by its translation into words. To communicate is to alter.

Bollas (1987) describes the advent of language as the most significant transformation for the developing child. It marks the change for the infant from making meaning out of their world through the medium of their primary caregiver, to being able to use language as a transformational object. Language allows the infant to enter a different world, 'facilitating the transition from deep enigmatic privacy towards the culture of the human village' (p. 35). It is the most significant transformation for the child as it allows them to find a meaning that is external to the primary caregiver. Language represents a new transformational object.

However, language cannot fully express experience as it is lived. What is lost in the translation from inter-subjective reality to verbal expression causes a split in the child's experience of self, and language becomes a double-edged sword. It allows the infant to begin to develop a narrative of their life but at the same time does not allow the experience of that life to be fully shared. What can be expressed is more easily accepted as real and so what is left unsaid can suffer alienation and become the 'nether domain of experience' (Bellaby-Langford 2001). How is experience known to be real if it is not expressed and shared with another? If a distressed child cannot put into words how they are feeling, adults will make their own assumptions about this and fill the void with their own interpretation of the child's possible experience. The potential is then for the child's experience to be changed and for the child to begin to mistrust their own feelings. This gives a menacing slant to Bollas's idea that now the child can speak for themselves without depending on the caregiver's interpretation. In fact the caregiver continues to interpret through validation or rejection of the child's efforts to put their feelings into words. In the transformation that Bollas is describing the child not only takes with them but continues to receive the influences of the inner world of their caregivers.

It seems that language creates an impersonal, abstract form of communication rather than the arguably more immediate and personal forms of communication that can be experienced through other domains of relatedness, such as the visual and physical. An infant's interpersonal knowledge is initially in the main unshareable and attuned to non-verbal behaviours. The advent of language changes that and the infant loses contact with the parts of their experience that cannot be verbally expressed. The child now learns to reduce experience so that it can be shared verbally. This process involves a condensation of their experience and the utilization of generalizations and the symbolic representation of events as they begin the lifelong process of describing themselves. These descriptions can be positive or negative. They can become 'bad girl', 'Mr Clumsy', 'good boy', 'Miss Clever'. Descriptions when repeated become labels which in turn become part of the family culture and subsequently a part of the individual's life story. Later in life these earlier, simplistic descriptions become more complex and appear as 'I am not good enough', 'I deserve to be punished', 'I will only be loved if I am clever/please others'. This process is in its very essence judgemental and it can easily become a given that the child is either good or bad. Those experiences that do not validate the accepted given become devalued and lost. This distortion of reality provides the soil for neurotic constructs (Stern 2000; Bellaby-Langford 2001). Stern describes how language introduces a hierarchy between behaviours and feelings, between what can be said and is therefore accountable and what cannot be expressed and is therefore deniable. Prior to language all of these had equal importance and could be equally owned.

Mollon (2003), in applying neuroscience to all this, suggests that the right hemisphere of the brain is the source of the true self, with the linguistic left hemisphere working with the pre-existing language and culture of the family to express the false or social self. This concept underpins Stern's work and the idea that the way a child develops in his or her use of language is shaped by the emotional and cultural environment in which they live.

Language is as important as affect and imagery in the central process of shaping the self. Kaufmann (1993) describes symbolic functioning as 'entrances to the self', with the self being 'both shaped and limited by language' (p. 273). Language reflects developmental history and the capacity for relationship. It represents part of individual and systemic history. The developmental needs of the self identified by Kohut (1977) – mirroring, idealization, twinship – begin to be met by verbal interactions as the child continues to develop.

Stern's 'slippage' between experience and words confronts practitioners in the therapy room. It comes from the past of both therapist and client. It comes from the personal and family relationship with language and its potential on the one hand to enhance, create, enrich and fulfil relational needs, and on the other to limit, distort, and destroy those relationships. If a therapeutic aim is to assist the client in naming their 'truth', this is done through a work of translation, empathic or interpretive, that parallels the early learning of language with its dilemmas of speaking 'truth', though a medium that cannot help but alter what it defines. Language is a conundrum. How different therapeutic models unpack this conundrum, how they use language and other forms of communication, and how they interpret meaning, forms the basis of the chapters that follow.

The words that make us: influences on the development of therapeutic language

Nicola Barden and Tina Williams

This chapter takes as its starting point the position that philosophy and psychotherapy both seek to understand meaning. Philosophy takes the big stage, the broad sweep, and tries to make sense of it; therapy takes the invisible inner world of the individual and offers a map, a cosmology of the unconscious (McLynn 1996). With Freud, hermeneutics transferred from religion into the secular world (Stevens 1983) just as philosophy found independence from the concept of God as part of the modern age. Philosophy is part of what forms the zeitgeist of the day, the backdrop against which all major therapeutic thinkers have developed their theories, whether explicitly aware of it or not. It affects the way of thinking, and what is thought about; it shapes how these thoughts can be expressed, and how they will be heard, through language, through writing and speaking. Linguists share the philosopher's dilemmas. Does language shape thinking? Does it reflect or create meaning? Is it constructed according to society or does it construct society? What follows is a conversation between philosophy, therapy and language, to draw out the relationship between them in a way that can illuminate and deepen an understanding of therapeutic communication.

The early days: an ontological background to Freud

Freud's achievements are situated in space and time, yet also form part of the universal desire to understand human behaviour. He had such a major impact on the beginning of modern psychotherapy that it is often imagined as springing forth fully formed from his brow, as

Athena sprang in adult shape from the head of her father, Zeus, the supreme deity in Greek mythology. In reality not only are there rich therapeutic traditions that existed before Freud, there are also many modern therapies in non-western cultures that continue to exist independently of his efforts.

Freud's work stands in a particular philosophical and cultural framework, as does the work of those who came after him, and it was informed by this framework, consciously or not. This framework influenced what he said and what he wrote, the language within which he could write, possibly even the thoughts that he could have. The use of therapeutic language needs to be informed by an understanding of this context, which can also help to clarify why some things are so hard to put into words and are perhaps better expressed through other media. Although the previous chapter looked at *how* language is learned, closer examination is necessary about *what* is learned along with language, the influences on its communicative role. There is no blank slate in language, no virgin ink for the pen.

The European outlook in the nineteenth century was influenced by Enlightenment ideals of rationalism, science and progress. The questions that dominated philosophical debate leading up to Freud's time, that would have influenced his mindset, focused on mind and its relationship to body, the nature of reality and the progress of the ideal of western civilization in personal, moral life as well as on the level of imperialism and the State. This individualistic outlook accorded well with and is likely to have contributed to the deeply intra-psychic emphasis of analysis.

McLeod (1997) suggests three main stages of cultural development in Europe and North America over this period. The traditional stage, with its emphasis on family life, religion and a static, morally certain life pattern, rested on stable, largely agrarian local communities. It might be said that limited communication opportunities during this period also slowed down development as changes could take a long time to migrate from one community to another. With the beginnings of the industrial revolution this traditional pattern moved into something more modernist. Urbanization and city living facilitated a rapid spread of ideas, and old religious certainties gave way to a belief in science, the individual and moral relativism. This in turn is now in flux, with post-modernism emphasizing the constructedness of internal and external worlds and thereby their openness to deconstruction. Information in the post-modern world is a means and an end, and McLeod (1997) posits that post-modernism itself represents a move away from the past but not necessarily towards a particular destination. This, as will be evidenced in Chapter 5, has led to a re-examination not only of culture but also of language.

The European world was heavily influenced by Greek philosophy and ideals. Greek language and mythology were taught in schools and universities in Freud's time, from Socrates' emphasis on the rational to Plato's divide between the material and the 'soul', or mind. Although Christianity in some senses held the body and soul together, Christian doctrine expecting the resurrection of both, it also put them in fundamental opposition to each other in this life, with their reconciliation waiting for another world. So the scene was ripe for what Koestler called the 'Cartesian catastrophe' (Whyte 1979) that marked the beginning of modern European philosophy and not only accepted the mind/matter split but also defined 'mind' as consciousness. This was a crucial word. The Greek 'mind' had been a broader concept, but this definition of mind as awareness meant for the first time that all the 'out-of-mindness' had to be put in a separate place, and so the concept of the unconscious mind entered European thought too. This is not to say that it was the first time that the unconscious had been thought about. St Augustine in the fourth century wrote, 'The mind is not large enough to contain itself: but where can that part of it be which it does not contain?' (Whyte 1979: 79). The sense of the unknowable in the mind has always been present, often explained by reference to a spiritual world in which symbols give some shape and identity to these forces. All religious motifs provide representations of good and evil, embodiments of the chaos and darkness experienced in the soul. They protect the integrity of the mind by lodging its inconsistencies and irrationalities in sprites, gods or forces of one sort or another that enable the confusion to be externalized, and instinctively represent the 'not-me' experience of unconscious motivations: 'I wasn't behaving like myself', 'Something just came over me', 'I just *had* to do it'. The locus of control is placed on the outside. Most religions are structured to meet this experience by offering external explanations of possession or spirit influence that are then amenable to repair through repentance or exorcism of some sort. So although the unconscious was very present, it was thought of in a different way, and one of Freud's great achievements was to recognize the unconscious as an internal country and begin to draw a map for it. He changed the meaning of the word, and the understanding of the mind with it.

What Freud did not seem aware of was the long tradition of thinking about mind that preceded him, and he protested strongly that he had no knowledge of those whose work clearly prefigured his own.

Koestler (1979) argues that the ability to not know what has gone before is as necessary to creative thinking as is the fact that much has indeed gone on before. 'For Freud to achieve what he did between 1895 and 1920 two conditions were necessary: that a long preparation should already have taken place and that he should himself be largely unaware of it, so that while unconsciously influenced by it he was free to make his own inferences from clinical observations' (p. x).

Words expressing consciousness and self-awareness came into European vocabulary during the seventeenth century. The language for unconscious mental processes came a little later, but was well under way by the mid-eighteenth century. Whyte interestingly reviews the way in which language at the time reflected the philo-sophical position of the country of origin. English culture was focused on 'politics and practicalities' and looked for the empirical evidence to support ideas of the unconscious; the French were acutely aware of society and brought subtlety and caution to the developing ideas; the Germanic countries were absorbed with introspection and the indi-vidual, and so brought systems to bear on the internal workings of the person. 'The German language tradition certainly displays most evidence both of an occasional intellectual obsession with the self-awareness of the individual, and later of a need to correct this by substituting, not a more balanced personal attitude, but a better theory of the mind' (Whyte 1979: 66).

Descartes took up the scientific end of the Cartesian mind/matter split and literally dreamt up a theory of rationalism. With a per-fect twist of irony his conviction that mathematical and scientific methods, that is, methods that need no recourse to the subjective senses, were the key to exploring truth came to him after a series of dramatic dreams, which he experienced as offering resolution to emo-tional torments through valuing the rational as the supreme code of existence – 'I think, therefore I am'. Freud interpreted those dreams as a crisis of conscience, and Descartes's resolution to ignore the emo-tional in favour of the rational is seen by many as a resolution of his personal conflicts writ large on a philosophical screen. Nevertheless, his emphasis on intellectual clarity had a profound influence, not least in reifying the conscious aspect of mind to the exclusion of the irrational in determining reality. While others encompassed a closer relationship between physical and mental states, Descartes championed their separation. Freud presented a profound challenge to Descartes as he intimately linked mind and matter through uncon-scious processes. Part of Freud's struggle was against an establishment that saw his ideas as far fetched or nonsensical because they had no place in the rational world view. To gain credibility he needed to speak to the medical valuing of rational and scientific proof, and this was his own value too from his medical training. Reading Freud's case studies is akin to observing a psychological dissection. He presents cases using clinical language where the reader is invited to observe and to learn from a dispassionate viewpoint, rather than to participate or identify. His impatience is apparent regarding more intuitive or spiritual approaches such as those of Jung, who wrote much more in the language of mysticism, being influenced by Eastern philosophies.

Descartes's Enlightenment thinking of course provoked responses that questioned the emphasis on rationality. The religious influence was still profound, and the mathematician and mystic, Pascal, brought to the foreground the necessary interplay between 'heart' and reason. Spinoza followed closely with his assertions that mind and body were the same thing, not in the literal sense that they could substitute for each other, but in the sense that the one could not exist without the other (Scruton 2002). They are both part of the whole system of being, and the concept of being is incomplete without both mind and body included in it. Then in 1781 came Kant's *Critique of Pure Reason*. Kant's parents were 'pietists', a reformist Lutheran movement emphasizing the sacredness of work, conscience and prayer (cited in Scruton 1997) which undoubtedly informed Kant's later views on the supreme nature of duty. For a man with little interest in power, his writings were influential far beyond their immediate sphere and time. While Descartes was concerned with truth and reason, Kant revered nature and freedom. Reality itself he saw as shaped by perception, which in turn came from experience.

Kant's mind was an active shaper of experience rather than a passive recipient of it. Life was not a jumble of unconnected events because the mind comprehended the relationships between experiences, past and present (Stapledon 1939). The experience itself was unknowable in a direct sense as it was always and only an apprehension of itself, conducted through the experiencer and thereby transformed as soon as apprehended. This philosophical point was to find a linguistic home in the later work of Lacan and the French analytic school for whom language was the signifier of the object – another way of saying that as soon as something is experienced on a conscious level it cannot be itself any more. To know that something has happened to you, you have to know that there is a 'you', that you are separate from those around you. The 'other' is a concept represented by a symbol, and the unique human system of symbols is language.

Language talks *about* something; it cannot talk the thing itself. However, Kant posited the 'thing-in-itself' as existing ultimately beyond perception. In this way he designed a bridge across mind/matter dualism at the same time as retaining it. He found understanding through and in the natural world, and his sense of meaning as residing in the connections between experiences was congruent with the work Freud was to begin on the structures and function of the mind. Desire as an amalgam of instinct and upbringing was familiar to both men, but to Kant this meant that as desire was either given or imposed it could not be freely chosen. Therefore to act from desire meant of necessity not to act from free will. Freedom can only come from actions unrelated to desire, to enable it to be chosen. Removing desire from the human picture leaves only rationality in its pure form, which is the form of moral law itself, or Kant's 'categorical imperative'. From this Kant reached a position that man was only free when acting from this imperative, or universal moral law, beyond a place that is either personal or desiring. Duty for duty's sake or, in more modern terms, following one's conscience (Singer 2001), is the greatest act of freedom. This philosophical background relates strongly to the language of therapy with its emphasis on the individual, on freedom and choice, and on finding a personal path that leads to a meaningful existence.

By the late eighteenth century, European philosophical debate was constellated around issues of meaning, morality and reality, often at a high level of abstraction. The nineteenth century was to take these thoughts even further, and it is possible to see the influence of Kant, Schopenhauer and Nietzsche in the writings of Freud, Jung and those who followed them. It was Hegel, however, who initially took the works of Kant forward; indeed Hegel regarded Kant as the starting point for modern German philosophy. Hegel also connected with some of the more romantic ideas of Goethe and Schiller, and had a strong sense of meaning existing in historical context – a concept later much used by Marx. Hegel's actual historical and cultural knowledge outside a European base limited the usefulness of his detailed ideas, but his overall point remained, that people exist in space and time, and the human condition changes from one era to another. Like Kant, what Hegel valued across all cultures, and the means by which he assessed their progress, was freedom and reason. The best society would be one in which all citizens consciously assented to rational standards of truth and goodness which, because they were universally based, would remove the discord between individual and state as both voluntarily have the same aim (Singer 1997). He believed that if people could give up desire and act from mind they would discover a universality of mind, resulting in the harmony of a shared nature based on reason. From this perspective Hegel disputed that there were as many realities as there were individuals, although he agreed that reality was constructed by the individual. The mind's goal was simply to know itself. Knowledge could only exist in communication with others, as there was no ultimately 'real thing'.

Language is therefore necessary as a means for one consciousness to communicate with another so that a self-consciousness may develop. 'Individual minds exist together, or they do not exist at all' (Singer 2001: 96). Echoes of this approach to knowing the self are heard clearly in the object-relations school; consider Winnicott's (1960a/ 1990: 39) phrase that there is 'no such thing as an infant', meaning that a baby cannot have an existence in isolation from maternal care. Winnicott meant by this not just physical dependency but that the existence of the baby as a person with a separate ego is created out of the interaction between the baby and the other.

Hegel's thoughts on communication go further in his emphasis on 'dialectic', or the move from thesis to antithesis and through to synthesis, so that opposites are reconciled until the reconciliation becomes a new thesis and the circle starts over again. This is very akin to Jung's (1916/1976) concept of the transcendent function, a term also used in higher mathematics (Samuels et al. 1986), in which a conscious attitude is complemented by an opposite unconscious one. This, if remaining entirely unknown to the individual, leads to domination by the known, and an imbalance in the whole personality. If the unconscious compensatory attitude can be contacted, however, and the two brought into relationship with each other, then 'the confrontation of the two positions generates a tension charged with energy and creates a living, third thing . . . a movement out of the suspension between opposites, a living birth that leads to a new level of being' (Jung 1916/1976: 298). Jung was not an admirer of Hegel, so it is interesting to see nevertheless how patterns of thinking co-exist in the atmosphere, whether or not one knows one is taking them in. Jung's transcendent function usually finds expression in a symbol – a dream or an image – that sparks its recognition and forms a turning point for the patient. Imagery and symbolism may be the only ways to communicate this elusive third; words are too specific.

Schopenhauer, born only 18 years after Hegel, was likewise influenced by Kant and Goethe and additionally had an interest in Indian thought, particularly the Hindu Upanishads. Ostensibly he opposed Hegel's views; Hegel supported Church and State, whereas Schopenhauer was an atheist and an individualist. Nevertheless, their philosophical systems bore similarities to each other (Janaway 1997), with Schopenhauer holding a bleaker, more depressive view of life overall as being something from which we seek release. He took refuge in Kant's view of the world as separated into appearance or things as they are perceived through the senses of the perceiver, and the thing-in-itself, existing outside of space and time and on the level of Plato's ideal forms, not reliant on the subject's experiencing of it. Schopenhauer placed his optimism in the experiencing of life at the level of the ideal.

Opposing mind/body dualism, Schopenhauer saw the body as activated by will, as an expression of it, necessary in order for will to exist, made necessary by the existence of will. He extended this to include the entire natural world which he believed to be a manifestation of will, here broadening the definition of will into a striving for life, and most fundamentally the continuation of life through which the concept of sexuality became central to the manifestation of will in the individual. 'Only the *will* is the *thing in itself* . . . It appears in every blindly acting force of nature, and also in the deliberate conduct of man, and the great difference between the two concerns only the degree of the manifestation, not the inner nature of what is manifest' (Schopenhauer, cited in Janaway 1997: 254). Daily existence is a struggle between base instinct and a higher intellectual plane, but there is another level of existence, the will and the thing-in-itself. This is beyond the pettiness of existence and is a constant reminder of and connection to the level of the ideal.

Jung acknowledged Schopenhauer's influence and thought his view of the world confused, passionate and evil: 'Here at last was someone who had courage for the insight that somehow the foundation of the world was not in the best of ways' (Jung, cited in Janaway 1997: 336). Freud held that he had not read Schopenhauer until long after his own arrival at the centrality of sexuality, so it is perhaps another interesting example of thoughts present in the air at that time, ready to be absorbed whether consciously or not.

Schopenhauer had a concept of the unconscious, and of repression as a method of coping with unwanted emotions. Nietzsche, who was born in Saxony in 1844, also had a strong sense of the unconscious, and as he was writing so close to Freud's own era, it is fair to assume not only that he would have influenced Freud in some way (although again Freud denied this) but also that the era itself was ripe for development of ideas of the unconscious; its time had come. The mind/body split and the alignment of mind with awareness had opened a space in which the irrational forces in the human being needed to be understood. To Nietzsche, the universe was full of energy, a source of creativity that was channelled through the conscious mind. Insight came through making the unconscious conscious, as it is the stronger of the two. Nietzsche used Schopenhauer's notion of the thing-in-itself, a sort of underlying unity in the universe, as a framework for his own thinking (Tanner 1997), focusing on fundamental and underlying structures that often had a darker, nihilistic and yet potentially appropriable energy to them. He also used Schopenhauer's concept of 'will to life' and transformed it into a Will to Power. This almost indefinable life-force focused often on survival, but as in the case of the martyr its key characteristic was a ruthless and overriding expansion of will, influence and efficacy over the self and the wider world. Indeed, despite Nietzsche's vocal distaste for the work of Hegel, an echo of the Hegelian concept of 'recognition' from the master slave dialectic was clearly present. Meaning and morality were products of this underlying principle of the will to power. It was perhaps a combination of the aspirational attitude and the semi-narcissistic bravado contained in this concept that led him towards the superman or 'Übermensch' image, unfettered and inspirational (Evans 1968). In the Will to Power he found a sort of answer to the meaning of existence in that the forcefulness of the push not only to survive, but to expand one's 'power', effect and influence over oneself and the wider world overrode all other questions, rendering them weak or subservient in comparison. What Nietzsche termed 'decadent' notions of harmony and morality, especially those set forth in Christianity, could positively damage survival and so could be enemies of life. It is not difficult to see how these ideas were appropriated and distorted by the German Reich after Nietzsche's death and led to his writings being ignored and misunderstood for a considerable time. Morality, where it was to be found, was individual rather than universal and in its uncritical guises subservient to more powerful and unconscious drives.

Themes from the times

Taking a step back from these particular influences on philosophical thinking in the two centuries leading up to Freud, what generic themes can be identified?

- The nature of reality. Is there a reality beyond what is perceived through the senses? If so, can we reach it? Does it affect us?
- Is there a universal morality or purpose which should guide behaviour and that, if followed, would create a harmonious state of affairs?
- What is the relationship between the body and the mind?
- What constitutes mind?
- How is the individual to live his or her life?

The individual runs like a thread through the middle of these questions: individual perceptions of reality, individual morality and meaning, individual bodies and minds, individuals in relationship to each other. Above the thread run the universals, the things-in-themselves, the ultimate realities existing independently from the individual. And underneath, the chaos, futility and irrationality from which the universals provide an escape. The themes are not dissimilar from the questions of religion: is there a purpose? Is there redemption? Can the forces of evil be overcome? Nor indeed are they unfamiliar within psychotherapy. How are we put together? Can our drives and instincts be manageable? Is there a higher function? Where is the individual in relation to otherness?

It might seem that religion, philosophy and therapy have much in common in the direction of their strivings, but with different viewing points and using different language to convey their meanings. Freud, in Vienna, was firmly located within an industrial, individualist, modern setting which, for all the strength of religious influence at the time, was secular in its thinking. His medical training reinforced the value placed on the scientific approach, and his spiritual leanings were grounded by the anti-Semitism that he and his family experienced (Jacobs 2003). Though he retained his Jewish identity he was aligned with Enlightenment values in viewing religious faith as a response to fear and ignorance (Lichteim 1972). Many other major thinkers were influenced by religion; Jung was perhaps an exception in maintaining a spiritual belief, but a childhood experience of religion nevertheless fundamentally shaped the questions that many went on to ask. Perhaps the advent of existential therapy is a sign of the closing gap between the triumvirate. This is not to say that Freud was simply pursuing religious or philosophical themes from an individualistic psychological position: the similarities can give an illusion of the universal and obscure what is particular.

Therapy as discussed in these pages undoubtedly refers to a particularly dominant European/North American discourse, focused on the

centrality of the individual, a culturally bound concept. The importance of family in China, for example, brings a whole different
emphasis to the relevance of the past as the memory of ancestors
plays an active part in present life. It is the family past that influences
the future, not a super-realm of ideals beyond perception. The individual is of much less interest. Of course the higher realm is populated
by significant gods and goddesses who perform necessary roles of protection, blessing and vengeance, requiring propitiation and attention.
But had analysis developed in China it would have had to have a very
different emphasis. It is interesting that therapeutic incursions into
that country are now American led and urban based, as a certain
amount of Americanization/Europeanization is necessary for the idea
to take hold and be experienced as relevant. Hong Kong, for years a
British colony with a broad multicultural experience, was open much
earlier to the growth of counselling and psychotherapy services,
although for some while still predominantly used by the non-Chinese
community.

Another significant development in the nineteenth century was the
publication of Darwin's *Origin of Species* (1859/1985), which was a
major influence in the post-Hegelian move to a more pragmatic philosophy which particularly suited the establishing zeitgeist of North
America. Not only did this remove the necessity of God from the
creation of the human species, it also questioned the assumption of
divine purpose or inevitable progress. If adaptation was a result of
random processes of selection that favoured survival, then adaptation
for survival rather than moral improvement was the leading rationale
for progress. Nor was each creature made perfect. Adaptations to
changing circumstances were constantly under way; even human
beings were adapting. The whole of life was a process. This developmental perspective fitted well with psychotherapy's approach to
change, and the survivalist strand in Freud's writing is clear to see. He
saw mind, like nature, as open to investigation, and the configuration
of internal objects open to change.

The frontier spirit in America confirmed a culture of individu-
alism and action; it's not who you are inside but what you *do*
that matters, as the girlfriend of the American comic book hero
Spiderman says to him. America was the one country Freud visited
outside of Europe when he was invited in 1909, with Jung, to deliver
a series of lectures. It was the place where many Jewish analysts went
to escape persecution in Nazi Germany and Austria. There is an argument that once the country itself was 'won', the frontier turned
inwards and the discovery of the human psyche was approached

in the same spirit as the land, as rich terrain for exploration and conquest.

Modern America was born out of the battle for control from the moment the Mayflower landed, man against nature. Out of this, and the eventual travails of the Civil War, came a more realistic approach: reality as determined by action, not perception. This was framed as 'applied philosophy' – beliefs are true if they work. Peirce (1905/1974) first named these pragmatic ideas. A mathematician and logician, his truth was 'what worked'. Perhaps because of Peirce's own exclusion from academia (his personal life was deemed unfitting), pragmatists became known for an anti-intellectual stance and a reliance on truth-through-feeling, embracing belief as well as logic (James 1902/1961) while retaining the emphasis on the practical. Belief, or truth, should be more than abstract theory; it should solve problems (Campbell 1995), and as such have a collective as well as an individual basis and relevance.

In this way pragmatists held views on social change, supporting Roosevelt's New Deal, for example, and leaning towards democracy as the pragmatic expression of a collective social endeavour. The new America was a land that needed people who could *do* – who could farm, build roads and railways. Action became a value, and knowledge was valuable inasmuch as it could contribute to change. The very newness of the country (in the frontier ethos of the time, that is; the country was transparently not new in every other sense) enabled a philosophical back to be turned on the old preoccupations of Europe about ultimate meaning. The pragmatic study of language emphasized ordinariness and utility – language was there to be used. Sentences were not things-in-themselves, but set in the context of speech, in the inter-relationship between speaker and listener. Speech was effective, language achieved things. Austen (1975) gave the example of the words of the marriage vow, 'I do'; they were not merely descriptive, they were an action in themselves, and this was the pragmatic thrust. This meant that pragmatism was generally disdained by Europeans such as Bertrand Russell, a British philosopher of the twentieth century who initially came under the influence of German idealism. Although he maintained a phenomenological aspect to his thinking he also moved much more closely to the concept of things existing independently of the object's perception of them. His realism, which was compatible with the American spirit, is summed up by Grayling (2002) as 'the thesis that the objects of experience are independent of experience of them', and his pluralism as 'the thesis that there are many independent things in the world' (pp. 34–5). On the one hand hard facts are beyond dispute; on the other, just because the earth looks flat does not mean that it is flat. Rorty (1991) is another of the better known, more modern pragmatists. He too rejected the notion of a single 'out-there' truth, but in a spirit of disinterest; the meaning of life would be found in the living of it; truth would be discovered through experience.

America has its own indigenous Native American Indian tribes, whose lives seemed to get swept up and spat out in the great conquering tide of settlement. The base of their philosophy, rooted in an appreciation of the indissoluble tie between humanity and nature, did not infiltrate what became mainstream ideology, which could hardly integrate what it had also denied and cast out. The naturalistic perspective, however, may be finding a more receptive and interested audience in the context of today's increased and overdue environmental awareness. Jung (1976) bemoaned the loss of beliefs incorporating gods of river and thunder. He valued the symbolism that could remind people of their small place in the larger natural world. Modern-day pragmatists recognize that truth does matter if an individual is oppressed; what works for one does not work for all.

This background makes some sense of the different trajectory of development undergone by counselling and psychotherapy in America. The analytic world guarded its roots by confining its practice to medically qualified persons. Psychoanalytically based practice in the States today is quite separate from counselling, which is firmly embedded in change-motivated models. America brought forth the great behavioural and cognitive practitioners like Skinner and Glasser, Ellis on rational emotive behaviour therapy, gestalt theorists such as Perls, body therapists like Lowen, who all focused on outcome. Their use of language reflects this. Words are used towards an end; sometimes they are not used at all. The emphasis is more on changing experience than inhabiting it, moving on rather then dwelling in. A great exception of course is Rogers (1951), for whom communicating experience to another is itself the healing experience, through the quality of the therapeutic relationship. Words are vehicles for relationship with the other and with the self. Listening became a core therapeutic activity, indicating presence and acceptance. Rogers posited that this is the core condition for change – the full and genuine inhabiting of the therapeutic space. Yet this too contains a fundamentally individualistic and optimistic philosophy, that progress can be made and things will get better.

Language

Language, as we saw in Chapter 1, is acquired as instinctively as any other naturally selected attribute in the Darwinian sense, and has its own role in the question of reality. It is not obviously discussed in earlier therapeutic writing because the study of language was itself not advanced enough at that point to be part of mainstream philosophy. But it did indeed subsequently take centre stage, for example in the works of Lacan, Sartre and Kristeva, and currently in the debates around narrative therapy. Yet as far back as 1912 a core debate began over the relationship of language to reality with what later became known as the Sapir–Whorf hypothesis on one hand, opposed by cognitive linguistics on the other. Sapir was sure that language was more than an objective method for communicating experience; it was part of what created experience, because the words available to describe an event already began to give the event a particular interpretation. This choice of words is made not only by the individual speaker but also by the philosophy of the surrounding community and culture which has linguistic 'habits' that essentially shape the choices available.

Take a simple example of greeting. In America the question 'how are you?' is responded to with a positive 'good', 'really well', 'great'; in the UK it is acceptable to say, 'not so bad', 'could be worse', 'OK'. Both responses mean the person is, on the level of polite enquiry at any rate, absolutely fine. But to reverse these and say 'great' in the UK would prompt an enquiry into what had just happened that was so wonderful, and to say 'not so bad' in the States would prompt an enquiry into what was the matter. Not only is this about different linguistic patterns but, argued Sapir and then his student, Whorf, it could also shape experience. If there are more words to describe low mood than high mood, might a people not inhabit the realm of low mood more as a matter of course, interpret their experience along a whole different spectrum, and concentrate more on unhappiness and depression than the high-mood group, rich in words for happiness and pleasure? Behind this is the assumption that interpretation affects experience, known as linguistic determinism, and that the interpretation itself depends on the words available, known as linguistic relativity. George Orwell used the concept in his novel *Nineteen Eighty-four* (1949/2000), when a totalitarian government planned to phase out the existing language of 'Oldspeak' and start again with 'Newspeak'. This would control the speaker's thoughts by limiting the vocabulary to include only approved words, so certain things would literally be unthinkable.

Pinker (1994) is a modern-day opponent of linguistic determinism, based on his view that as language is an instinct it is fundamentally universal, and thought is not directly linked to language
but has a language of its own that he calls 'mentalese'. So while he
does not deny that different languages have different emphasis and
specialities, he sees these as reflective rather than formative of the
realities of that culture, and without effect on the capacity to have
thoughts outside of the language constraint. He gives the example of
Bloom's experiments on Chinese speakers. The Chinese language
has no formula for the subjunctive so cannot in that way express
something 'counterfactual', that is, *if* X, *then* Y. Because they were
unable to form such sentences Bloom concluded that 'Chinese language renders its speakers unable to entertain hypothetical false
worlds without great mental effort' (Pinker 1994: 66). This, as Pinker
comments, is patently ridiculous, and made obviously so by subsequent and improved experiments. Pinker's sticking point is that
experience is mediated by thought rather than language, and thinking is not underpinned by linguistics. Language subsequently communicates the thought, so communication, but not the experience
itself, may be limited or enhanced by the peculiarities of a particular
language.

The significant flaw in the Sapir–Whorf hypothesis is surely that
language arises out of communities and so is formed by them. At
the very least they inform each other – there is no one-way traffic.
Language continually changes, and limitations imposed by it are open
to development. On the other side, there is something self-fulfilling
about always expecting what has always been there, and language can
draw attention to some areas in preference to others. The use of pronouns is a useful example. In German and French the speaker must
continually make decisions about the nature of their relationship to
the person they are speaking to, since they must address them with
either the informal '*du*' or '*tu*', or the formal '*Sie*' or '*vous*', whereas in
English 'you' will cover both. An awareness of social relations is thus
built into the language. However, it could not be argued that the UK is
a country free from consciousness of social relationships as a result;
indeed, its class consciousness is arguably greater than either France or
Germany's. Thought will find its way through to expression, though it
might be true that the construction of each language makes some
thoughts more straightforward to express, and possibly to have, than
others. Communication, written or spoken, stimulates the mind. Or,
as a dyslexic speaker at a conference about thought and language put
it when talking about the written word, 'Thought is not necessarily

hindered by reading and writing difficulties, but the availability of things to think about is' (Jansons 1988: 505).

Conclusion

Psychotherapy and philosophy have language in common. Whether language shapes thinking, or thought can exist independently of language, without a shared symbolic system there is no common currency with which to exchange, store and build on these thoughts. Without a language, psychotherapy and philosophy would not exist.

The twentieth-century philosopher, Wittgenstein (1922/1963), explored the relationship of philosophy to language. He described philosophical propositions and questions as difficulties in understanding language. If the logic of language could be grasped and applied then basic life concepts could be identified. By gaining a clear understanding of how language works, reality could be explained. It is not the mystery of the world that prevents understanding but the language used to interpret it. Things are as language says they are, which gives great power to the dominant linguistic culture in shaping reality.

Wittgenstein later moved away from this essentialist view in his posthumously published work, *Philosophical Investigations* (1958). Here he wrote of philosophy being concerned with possibilities rather than the actual; language did not explain, but described. It is contextual, and takes on the history and prejudices of its context. Language lives in the story of its originating culture, and philosophy is the study of what underpins a culture, its guiding principles. Language and philosophy are formed from and by each other. And this is the same language that is available for the construction of therapeutic theories, for clients to express themselves, and for therapists to understand them.

The whole of language works as a result of context. Sentences are made through applying rules to words. Where there is a verb, a noun will be close by. If the verb is to throw, a moveable object is anticipated. Words are grouped according to similarities and differences: things that can be thrown and things that are fixed. Language is potentially infinite but actually very precise. Recognizing the connection between language, therapy and philosophy is an essential for any therapist who, in endeavouring to remain open and responsive to their clients, understands that they also need to remain open and questioning of their world, their beliefs and, most importantly, to the way they use language to communicate them.

CHAPTER 3

Language in therapy: words and symbols across theoretical frameworks

Nicola Barden and Tina Williams

This chapter aims to give an overview of the role of words and symbols across the different therapies as they have grown into being over the last 150 years. It is of necessity a very brief summary, but it is possible to trace some common themes, which will be gathered together at the end.

Freud

Psychoanalysis provided the foundation for modern psychotherapy, and Freud's forensic approach to psychology, that is, seeking the causes underlying any disturbance, determined his approach to symbolization. Unconscious actions – dreams, slips of the tongue, 'hysterical' symptoms – signified repressed material requiring recognition and release. Symbols simply meant one thing standing in for another. The repressed item they stood for was as yet unknown in that it resided in the unconscious, whereas the symbols were familiar, the mystery being in their relationship to the unconscious material. The task of the analyst in relationship to symbolic expression therefore was no different to any other expression, that is, to uncover the repressed material, which is often related to wish fulfilment, underneath.

Symbols can be part of the symptom. Freud (1926/1959: 90) gave the example of how the act of writing could assume the significance of sex through the link with fluid coming out of a tube, and this may make someone unable to put pen to paper. Although the symptom may be problematic, Freud saw it as essential that anxiety should have an outlet, and so symbols were functional in returning the organism into some sort of workable balance. Better not to write, perhaps, than to be overcome with anxiety relating to repressed sexual phantasies.

Freud's attitude to symbols was twofold. First, they possessed meaning unique to the individual; second, certain symbolic themes were ubiquitous. The two attributes were not exclusive – the pen in the earlier example could possess a particular meaning for the client, for example if it was the pen their father wrote with, and at the same time the sexual allusion of the nib and the ink could be relevant in any circumstance. Thus the therapist needs to work with both the client's *associations* to the symbol, and their own *interpretations* of it.

The relation of the dream element to its portrayal in the dream tended to be part object, allusion or 'plastic portrayal' (Freud 1916/ 1963: 151). Mostly reliant on imagery, dreams could also use words, or a dream element in itself could be standing in for a word. Sometimes these would be specific to the language of the age. A woman falling down could be a reference to a 'fallen woman' in the sense of sexual impropriety (Freud 1900a/1953: 202); a man in a tower could be seen as 'towering above' others (Freud 1900b/1953: 342). At other times the symbol could be culturally specific. A dream figure of a woman in a white robe in England may have associations with purity, virginity, perhaps bridal ceremonies; in China white is the colour of mourning, and would be associated very differently, with death and loss and funerals. Other symbols would cross culture and time as being universally relevant, and Freud paid particular attention to these.

Freud put symbolic understanding to use primarily in the interpretation of dreams. This was by no means exclusive: he saw symbolism in myths and fairy tales, jokes and stories. But as dreams were so utterly out of the conscious control of the dreamer Freud valued them as offering unparalleled access to the unconscious, if only they could be deciphered. Dreams at the time were viewed with detachment in the scientific community as a purely physical process with no particular meaning. Lay analysis was confined to a number of 'dream-interpretation' books which offered standard decoding for dreamed-of objects, or alternatively looked for analogous situations to those in the dream. Freud however saw dreaming as a mental act, capable of being given meaning. The dreamer did not need to know the collective meaning of the symbol: it was the unconscious that knew it, and the unconscious that threw it up as dream or allusion or slip of the tongue. Freud saw the different types of symbolization shading into each other, from replacement to representation to allusion. His diagnostic approach, seeing them as purposive, bound them into a sufficiently coherent category.

Freud observed a small but fundamental number of themes persistently represented in dreams: the human body, the family, birth and death, nakedness and sex. Although dismissive of conventional dream books and insistent on the analyst's responsibility to know the patient and engage in the patient's associations with dream material, his observation of this persistence led him to create his own guide to dream symbolism, albeit on a complex level intimately related to his theories of human development. He believed these symbolic connections to be deeply rooted in the past: 'Things that are symbolically connected today were probably united in prehistoric times by conceptual and linguistic identity' (Freud 1900b/1953: 352). He saw the therapist as having these interpretations available to use with the patient if the individual associations of the patient confirmed them. A house, then, would represent the human figure as a whole; with smooth walls it would be a male, with balconies a female. Emperors, kings, queens, were parents; small animals and vermin, siblings. Water was most often connected with birth; departures such as train journeys with death. Clothes and uniforms indicated their reverse, nakedness. And a great number of symbols were used in connection with sexual life. Almost any long or upstanding shape could represent the male genital – sticks, umbrellas, trees – as could penetrating objects like knives or spears, extendable items like pencils or lamps, things that rise up like balloons or flying itself, things that emit water like taps and fountains. Female genitals took the form of objects that enclosed a hollow space that could take something into itself – bottles, boxes, jewel cases, valleys; cupboards and rooms were the uterus; the entrance to the vagina, a mouth, doors, gates. Breasts could be apples, pears, peaches. Masturbation could be represented by sliding or gliding actions, or playing for example the piano; intercourse by dancing, riding, threatening with weapons (Freud 1916/1963). Freud's dream-world was soaked in sexuality, in the libido that he saw dominating all unconscious life. As the '*royal road to a knowledge of the unconscious*' (Freud 1900b/1953: 608), it could hardly be otherwise.

The 'Wolf Man' (Freud 1918/1995) provides a good example of a case of a dream analysis in which classical Freudian sexual interpretation of symbols plays a large part. It also demonstrates the creativity of Freud's approach. The man concerned was a young Russian who saw Freud from 1910 to 1914. The dream was recounted quite early in the analysis, and was interpreted gradually over the years. It occurred when the client was 4 or 5 years old. In the dream he was in bed at night looking out of the window towards an old walnut tree. In the tree sat six or seven motionless white wolves. The window opened.

The dreamer screamed in terror of being eaten by the wolves, and woke up.

Freud worked through his patient's associations with various aspects of the dream. The wolves brought to mind a folk story about a tailor pulling off a wolf's tail while defending himself, which Freud associated with castration. The patient recalled a story, 'The Wolf and the Seven Little Goats', which accounted for the numbers. What the patient noticed most was the complete stillness and attentiveness of the wolves, and the sense of reality in the dream. Freud took this as an indication that something in the dream did originate in reality, the actual event having been forgotten or repressed and translated into the dream. The wolves and the tree and the night were therefore symbols for something that survived in the patient's psyche, but remained in disguise. Freud took the wolves' attentiveness and still-ness to be a transposition of the patient's own state of watchfulness, and assumed he had seen something with opposite qualities that was lively and disturbing, that he should not have seen, and that in some way was linked to castration, the wolf's loss of its tail. Freud surmised, after lengthy discussion with the patient and further associations, that as a very small child he had witnessed his parents in intercourse, and later associated his desire for his father as leading to castration if fulfilled, having seen that his mother did not posses a penis. The wolves represented the frightening father and the castrated mother. Freud was all too aware how fanciful such an explanation might seem to his audience. At this stage in his account he wrote, 'I have now reached the point at which I must abandon the support I have hitherto had from the course of the analysis. I am afraid it will also be the point at which the reader's belief will abandon me' (Freud 1918/1995: 410). Freud combined his own questions and thoughts with the patient's associations and memories to propose a radical interpretation consistent with his central formula of the Oedipus complex. A wolf may not be a wolf. Although, as Freud is purported to have said later, sometimes a cigar is just a cigar.

Klein and Bion

For Klein, play linked physical to mental life through the mechanism of unconscious phantasy (Hinshelwood 1991). In her efforts to understand the inner world she closely observed infants and young children and pioneered the use of play as a therapeutic intervention, much as Freud pioneered dreamwork. She drew a picture of a chaotic, intense world where infants experienced either enormous bliss or great terror, rapturous oneness with the mother or total abandonment by her, as a result of their complete physical dependency and undeveloped egos. All these fears were concentrated on the body, as mental life was almost entirely mediated through physical experience: feeding, being held, being changed, and so on, and conversely through hunger, cold and discomfort. Thus bodily parts were the first symbols. Unlike Freud, Klein (1930/1988) believed that children had an instinctual knowledge of the genital organs so there was no 'discovery' of the penis. Initially these, as with all things, were part rather than whole objects, and were to be found all together in the body of the mother. The breast was the object of greatest significance to the infant, and it came to represent not only the mother but a 'symbol of all goodness, love and security' (Weininger 1992: 54), of the understanding that comprises the first experience of communication: 'Understanding is felt to belong to the containing breast: the nipple provides the template for words which link it to the baby' (Segal 1992: 119).

Phantasy, with its use of symbols, was to Klein essential in order for the infant to manage the anxiety that threatened to overwhelm it. 'Symbol formation is an activity of the ego attempting to deal with the anxieties stirred by its relation to the object and is generated primarily by the fear of bad objects and the fear of the loss or inaccessibility of good objects' (Segal 1986: 52). What was frightening related not only the external world but also to the internal one – the baby's own feelings that threatened to engulf it, making it fearful of destroying others with the force of them, or of making others retaliate. If an external representation can be found for an internal persecutory object, the infant is both relieved of the internal persecution and has an opportunity to let the object become 'good' again. Although the *feelings* are projected onto the breast, which acts as a symbolic container for them, the breast is still believed by the infant to *literally* contain the feelings. So for example an unsatisfying feed at the breast means the child experiences it as a withholding, persecutory object, entirely separate from the good-feed breast of a couple of hours previously. It holds not only the experience of the bad feed but also the hatred felt by the infant towards it as the withholding object. When the infant is next offered the breast for a feed it may turn away and refuse it as it still holds all this badness and is therefore a fearful object, the desired breast being deemed to be entirely separate and elsewhere. If the mother can tolerate this and provide a good feed nevertheless, the breast returns to being a good object full of loving feelings, and the infant is relieved that it has not been able to destroy goodness despite its hatred. Segal (1986) calls these 'symbolic equations', where the symbol is felt to be the thing itself and not a substitute for it. Regression to this early phase can be observed in psychosis, where the 'as-if-ness' of an experience is absent. Jung (1963) referred to a young woman he worked with in a hospital who believed herself to live on the moon, and would look in the night sky for her home. Jung spoke with her as if she did in fact live on the moon, as in his view psychic reality held greater substance than externally verifiable reality.

Bion, who was analysed by Klein, saw that without the capacity to use symbols the relationship between the internal and the external world would inevitably be distorted. Psychosis attacked the capacity to make links between inside and outside – fundamentally attacking the capacity to think. This makes it impossible to contain difference within the same object, or to create something new out of opposing forces without having to destroy one of them. 'Consequently the formation of symbols, which depends for its therapeutic effect on the ability to bring together two objects so that their resemblance is made manifest, yet their difference left unimpaired, now becomes difficult' (Bion 1967: 50). The world inside cannot accommodate the world outside and so becomes isolated from it and continues in a state of part-object relationships. 'The consequences for the patient are that he now moves, not in a world of dreams, but in a world of objects that are normally the furniture of dreams' (p. 52).

As the ego matures, in Kleinian terms the infant progresses towards the depressive position. In this it can grasp that the good and the bad are both from the same breast and that this breast, or mother, exists independently of the infant's attacks or phantasies. Here the infant progresses from symbolic equation into symbolism proper. There is a conscious understanding that there is a thing, that the thing functions as a symbol, and that there is a person for whom the one represents the other. Reaching this stage requires a complex piece of emotional and psychological development which itself requires the use of symbols in phantasy life. Klein (1930/1988) underlines how symbols are present from the very start and are an integral part of the development of self. As well as managing anxiety they establish curiosity as they bring the individual into the world of the not-me and assist in engagement with it: 'not only does symbolism come to be the foundation of all phantasy and sublimation but, more than that, it is the basis of the subject's relation to the outside world and to reality in general' (p. 221).

Klein worked with children through the medium of play, which she saw as equivalent to dream life in terms of exposing unconscious phantasies. Play offered direct symbolization through using objects, akin to words in adult life. If the meaning of the symbols could be interpreted and transferred from the act of play into words, the under- lying anxieties were addressed and the child was able to make sense of the not-understood feelings that engulfed them. Bion emphasized the containment of anxiety which came about through being able to think about and put into words the emotional truth of a situation. Bion and Klein both saw words as vital links between mother and child and, in the consulting room, between analyst and patient. Words created a bridge at the same time as resting on borders; the word 'hello' meets, greets and simultaneously creates an anticipation of farewell. Words do not achieve the one-ness that the infant phantasizes, but they enable separateness to be borne by facilitating attachments that can be sustained symbolically.

The ability to use symbols in this way depends on the ability to retain an image of something when it is absent. It is difficult to know exactly when this happens for an infant, but it slowly coalesces and becomes more robust with experience. There is some evidence that babies only a few days old can count and notice a change in sequence, which indicates a very early memory for absent objects. Better known is the hide-and-seek game that adults play with small children in which they grow from being quite unaware of an object if it is out of sight to being able to go back and find it, confident that it will be where it was left. In this way the child copes with the absent mother, learning to hold her in mind, and to experience her containment even in her absence.

The ability to symbolize is seen by Klein (1930/1988), and by the object-relations theorists, as essential to adult life: the infant is learn- ing an essential survival and developmental skill. All the talent of sublimation relies on the capacity to allow one thing to stand in for another so that energy can move from one field into another. Authors, painters, musicians use their craft to transfer affect: a paint- ing is never just a copy of an image; it is imbued with the meaning of the image to the artist. Psychological content finds expression and a home at some remove from the original moment. 'The creative artist makes full use of symbols; and the more they serve to express the conflicts between love and hate, between destructiveness and repar- ation, between life and death instincts, the more they approach the universal form'. Here Klein draws on a similar idea to Jung, of collect- ive, universal, deeply unconscious human themes or experiences that find representation in the external world. She goes on to say, '[The artist] thus condenses the variety of infantile symbols, while drawing on the full force of emotions and phantasies which are expressed in them' (Klein 1963/1984: 299). Without symbolism the inner world would remain primitive and incommunicable. Fear would remain fear – a 'beta element' in Bion's structure, which can be ejected or projected but as a beta element is untransformed and remains a permanent threat. Symbolization transforms the beta into 'alpha' elements, through dreaming or thinking or putting into words. Fear therefore finds a place in the external world, becoming sharable and available to amelioration. Symbols allow sense to be made of the world.

Winnicott

Human relationships thus rely on the capacity to symbolize in the most elemental sense of establishing a self and a not-self. Winnicott (1963/1990), following Klein, saw symbolization as necessary for establishing a temporal sense of self in the world as the infant is able to keep the mother in mind during an absence and to expect her return. This is observable concretely in the 'dropping game' that infants love to play, where an object can be taken away and made to reappear, and the expectation of its reappearance grows with the confidence of its continuing existence even when out of sight (Winnicott 1954/1992). Symbolism facilitates the capacity to be alone, which is developed by periods of being alone with the mother, or with things that can represent being with the mother – a cot, or pram. 'The capacity to be alone depends on the existence of a good object in the psychic reality of the individual' (Winnicott 1958/1990: 31-2). Winnicott (1951/1992) emphasized the importance of 'transitional objects' for the development of the space between inner and outer, self and other. This is the space beyond instinct and the body, before whole object relating; beyond thumb sucking but before the teddy bear. Often sensate, the transitional phenomenon can be the sound of the infant's own babbling, or the feel of the corner of a blanket held while nursing. It is the beginning of symbol formation, a part-object not-self, made possible by a secure environment. The need for symbols is not grown out of, but remains a creative part of adult life and communication. Winnicott (1960b/1990) gives an example of a 7-year-old boy who used string to illustrate his separation anxiety relating to his mother, winding the string round tables and chairs to tie them to each other. When he was enabled to put his anxieties into words he no longer needed to use the string; the word-symbols would do instead, and then he could be responded to, and his fear could change. Therapy is a field in which this transformation is constantly occurring; from the action, or non-verbal communication, or the dream, to the word, from the unconscious to the conscious.

Jung

Winnicott and Bion both saw the central place of this symbol-making capacity in adult creativity – in the arts, in scientific invention, religion and myth. In this they both drew on the work of Carl Jung, an erstwhile disciple of Freud's until the two men parted irrevocably in disagreements over issues of sexuality and spirituality. Jung developed a rather different approach to symbols. Unlike Freud, he differentiated between what he called signs and symbols. By signs he meant one thing standing in as a representation of another – what Freud would have termed a symbol. At a basic level a sign is the very function of language – we can say 'dog' and conjure up a reliable and roughly shared image of a canine animal, without needing the dog to be present to testify to its existence. Less descriptive, but still with meanings based on equivalences, were signs that allowed one thing to act as a symbol of another, like an umbrella for a penis, or a wardrobe for the womb. A step further were signs that have a commonly under-stood meaning, without actually referring to their object, for example a trademark or logo. All these 'are not symbols. They are signs, and they do no more than denote the objects to which they are attached' (Jung 1978: 3).

Symbols, however, while they may be perfectly ordinary words or images, in Jungian psychology apply themselves to something that is not apparent, something often not entirely known or understood, 'thus a word or an image is symbolic when it implies something more than its obvious and immediate meaning' (Jung 1978: 4). Symbols may be produced consciously, or unconsciously as in dreams. They are individual and collective. The cross is an example given by Jung of a true symbol. On one level it denotes a wooden structure, an ancient method of execution. On another it is a symbol of resurrection, suffer-ing, redemption, an entire moral and religious code and 2000 years of history. It is living and evolving; the meaning has never become fixed. The cross is a sign transformed into a symbol:

Every view which interprets the symbolic expression as an analogue or an abbreviated design for a known thing is semiotic. A view which interprets the symbolic expressions as the best possible formulation of a relatively unknown thing, which for that reason cannot be more clearly or characteristically represented, is symbolic. A view which interprets the symbolic expression as an intentional paraphrase, or transmogrification of a known thing is allegoric.

(Jung 1923: 601)

While Freud emphasized the unique place of dreams in providing access to unconscious complexes through the use of free association to dream material, Jung viewed free association as a technique that could be more widely used in relation to pictures, meditation and even conversation. The dream to Jung had a different unique quality: it *was* the expression of the unconscious. If dreams were clearer, they would be memories. His dreams did not need deciphering using symbols as a sort of code; they were already perfectly formed as an expression of unconscious life, and could literally reveal what the dreamer did not know for themselves. For this reason Jung eschewed dream books, although he did acknowledge common themes – flying, falling, running and getting nowhere, being lost or naked. He recommended that all motifs were considered in the framework of the original dreamer.

In Jungian dream analysis both the therapist and the patient may make associations to the dream, and the therapist benefits from as wide a cultural education as possible so that he or she may be able to see collective allusions of which the dreamer is unaware, a process known as amplification. 'But if we are to see things in their right perspective, we need to understand the past of man as well as his present. That is why an understanding of myths and symbols is of essential importance' (Jung 1978: 45). What is relevant to the case, however, only the dreamer can decide. Jung encouraged his students to learn everything they could about symbols, and then forget it all when meeting with the individual patient. Hillman (1977) uses the analogy of mining to describe working with words and symbols. Mining occurred before modern technology, as dreams and images were understood before modern psychology. But 'what does help mining is an eye attuned to the dark' (p. 82).

Jung (1978: 14) illustrated the importance of context through an altarpiece by Campin, a fifteenth-century Flemish artist, depicting a nun and a monk kneeling before an open door with a key in the lock. While this is open to a sexual interpretation, religious symbolism of the time would equally have intended the door to be seen as hope, the lock as charity and the key as the longing for God. The desire could be more spiritual than carnal. Jung valued the spiritual in life, believing people lived symbolically as well as symptomatically (Whitmont 1978).

For Jung the purpose of living was to become most fully oneself, to 'individuate'. To illustrate what he meant by this he used the medieval metaphor of alchemy, or the struggle to combine various elements into a substance that would form pure gold. A spiritual as well as a material quest, Jung found in the analogy a perfect illustration for the need for one element to cease to be in its old form in order for another to come into existence and in this sense for psychic death to occur, to release attachment to the status quo, in order for life to continue. Stasis smothered creativity and the psyche needed to be in a perpetual state of motion, like a pendulum swinging from one extreme to the other, the aim being not to stop in the middle but to allow movement to continue freely and life energy to circulate. The purpose of an individual's dream life, as of their waking life, was the move towards individuation (von Franz 1978).

As life's central struggle, individuation was represented in universal motifs, played out with cultural specificity but following recognizable themes. These motifs are found in fairy tales, myths, folklore, religious stories. They are often called 'archetypal'. For Jung, archetypes were the content of the collective unconscious, archaic patterns marking universal themes, sometimes referred to as 'psychic instincts'. They are often confused with the symbols that illustrate the themes, but they stand behind and beyond this, primitive, primordial, essential. To return to the image of the cross, a numinous symbol, this is not an archetype in itself, but the story of Christ can be seen as part of the hero myth found across all cultures and in many religions – a miraculous but humble birth, early proof of superhuman abilities, a triumphant struggle over the forces of evil, fallibility, fall through betrayal or heroic sacrifice, leading to death (Henderson 1978). These themes tell the story of the struggle of the self to realize itself, the need to develop the ego so that the self can be brought into relationship with the world, dying to itself and rising again in the repeated process of incarnation. The self is an archetype and finds expression through motifs like the hero, and Jungian analysis looks to perceive and support these themes as they appear in the dreams, thoughts and actions of the patient. In this way symbols are not only as important as words but in some ways are more profound. They are capable of containing the deepest themes, some that perhaps cannot be spoken about since they can only be adequately described indirectly, as it required the Taj Mahal to speak of grief, or a wreath of poppies to capture the heroism and loss of war.

Jung did not look for symbols to lead him somewhere else but sought rather to enter the symbol and discover its transforming power. Oliver Sachs (1985) tells the moving story of 'Jimmie', a man afflicted by Korsakov's syndrome, a destruction of long- and short-term memory caused by alcohol abuse. His life continually puzzled him as he had no context for it, and discontent swamped every action as achievement was temporary, forgotten the next day, but the desire for meaning and purpose remained strong. Unexpectedly the Catholic Mass provided a ritual that absorbed and focused him, where he would attend with calm and concentration. Sachs postulates there was something in the community and ritual of the Mass that held Jimmie in a sort of continuity with himself, no longer wandering unattached in the world. A similar calm would come over him when listening to music or working in the hospital garden. Jungians might attach an archetypal significance to the ritual of the Mass, present in the collective unconscious which was part of Jimmie's psyche, a containing element that did not rely on temporal awareness. On attending chapel Jimmie literally entered a symbolic representation of the archetype in a way that made it once more accessible to him through a portal that did not require conscious memory.

Lacan

The Jungian ability to inhabit symbols in this deep way later provided a lead into the work of arts (art, drama, music, dance) therapists, and indeed Jung worked pictorially as well as with words. But returning to words, Jacques Lacan is probably the most significant post-Freudian contributor to the field of psychoanalysis and linguistics. Speech, according to Lacan, is what gives 'man' his consciousness and therefore his reality, because it means that desire can be mediated, and thought about. Lacan saw the unconscious itself as structured like a language. Words, or 'signifiers', gain meaning through their relationship of similarity or difference to each other, just as the world of the infant is made up of a space structured by difference and opposition (Macey 1988), most fundamentally sexual difference. The infant learns its 'place' through its relationship with this structure, just as words find their sense through their context in a sentence. The child is no more omnipotent or powerful than the word is: 'The psycho-analytic experience has rediscovered in man the imperative of the Word as the law that has formed him in its image' (Lacan 1979: 57).

Lacan viewed language as essentially duplicitous. Language plays tricks on the user – or rather the user plays a trick on themselves through language. The subject believes in their authorship of the language they speak, but Lacan held that it was actually the other way round – that language creates the subject and their world. By describing objects, emotions and events through language they are given a form that allows them to be shared in the present and the past and also into the future. Yet just as an artist cannot make a real person by drawing an imaginary face, so the process of creation through the use of language cannot make something real – it can just lead to a belief that it is real. The word cannot equal the thing it describes; it refers to it, and the alignment can never be perfect: 'The structure of language always introduces an element of fiction' (Lacan, cited in Macey 1988: 255). This is the 'trick', and it leaves the question, what is real? In the context of the world that is created through language, nothing is real. Experience is a combination of images plus the language that is used to describe them.

Lacan concluded that there was in fact a 'real' state of being (reflecting a Hegelian influence) but that it had been lost touch with and could not be conveyed through language. This loss was the root of neurotic suffering. The acquisition of language itself necessitated the loss of the unity with the world, a unity that he posited was experienced by new-born infants. The newborn has a sense of oneness with the world, a lack of boundaries or distinction between itself and the world into which it is born, indeed as if it had not been born and was still in the womb, in a symbiotic relationship with the universe. Lacan described a stage where the child begins to develop a sense of separateness – a 'mirror' stage, the child literally being able to recognize its image in the mirror. With this recognition of separateness and of its own ego the child loses its initial sense of merger with the environment and becomes aware that another (the mother/carer) wants the child and that the child in turn also wants this other. The child now sees itself as whole again but only because it is in relation with the other – the two together make a whole. The image that the child sees in the mirror is illusory and the illusion is shattered as the child enters into the world of language. Irigaray (1977/1991) was to take this further and consider that the mirroring gaze of the mother, affecting as it did infant growth and development, would be visible through the language of the child: 'Distortions of language can . . . be related to a distortion of the specular experience' (p. 81). As it learns to describe itself as 'I' and begins to discover the symbolic and social order of the world it is impossible for the infant to maintain the illusion of one-ness with its carer/mother. Lacan sees this as a simultaneous loss of unity *and* the sense of an even deeper desire for what we once knew as real, as the truths of our existence.

It is this gap, this absence, that is held in the unconscious and continually seeks fulfillment. This for Lacan is the basis of problems and difficulties in life. Both the ego from the 'imaginary' realm and the 'I' from the symbolic are false – what is commonly supposed to be identity is false. However, seeking the truth runs counter to the human framework as it exposes the unbearable realization of the falseness of the world.

Lacan translated Freud's writings into French and offered a closely related but alternative psychoanalytic model, but he also subtly trans-formed some of Freud's ideas. For Lacan, Freud's eros is understood as the underlying desire for the real; the Oedipal story is represented by the role language has in facilitating separation from the mother and as such takes the role of the father. The unconscious contains the unbearable desire for truth. The infamous Freudian slip illustrates that the truth is expressed through what is actually said rather than the spirit of what is said (Gallop 1984); post-Lacanian therapy has as its goal not the psyche but the letter. For Lacan language was a symbolic bridge between two realms – the real and the imaginary.

The corollary of Lacan's theories is that emotional relationships have a linguistic structure which is initially learnt in families, just like a language, without conscious awareness. The narrative style of the adult reflects the attachment patterns of the child (Bowlby 1997; Holmes 2001). The way in which the self is articulated is of central importance in therapy. Different voices of the self are presented in psychotherapy through types of speech (Georgaca 2001). For example, Forness-Bennett (1997) referred to four senses of 'I': the *analytic self*, concerned with the relationship between language and experience; the *narrative self*, which puts the self into the context of the story being told; the *pragmatic frame*, which distinguishes 'I' as the person telling the narrative; and the *reflexive self*, the person looking at them-selves objectively and reflecting on the meaning of the story for them. The reflexive 'I' brings together and holds the other selves and is based on the person's early experience of mirroring in building their inner or representational worlds. The reflexive function is indicative of the person's capacity to protect themselves psychologically and can be seen as the goal of therapy (Holmes 2001). However, it has

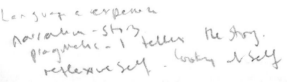

been argued that a fluent narrative self with a healthy interplay between the different voices is even more important (Georgaca 2001).

It is clear that being sensitive to the predominant linguistic frame that the client uses is a significant aspect of forming a therapeutic working alliance, along with developing empathic attunement with the client and understanding the client's pattern of contact in relationship with self and other – these are all fundamental therapeutic elements.

Lacan's theories can lead to the feeling that life itself is just a fiction, a story made up for comfort in the face of the state of continual misunderstanding in which life is lived, as with the main character in Gaarder's novel *Sophie's World* (1968), who believed herself to be real but all the time was only a character in a story. Everything is an illusion, maintained by a continuing belief in it. Lacan admired the surrealists, and their influence is clear in his writing; and the surrealists admired Freud (who once had a meeting with Salvador Dali) for his subversiveness. Freud was rather less keen on the surrealists as he saw his own work embedded firmly in the scientific rationalism of nineteenth- and twentieth-century Europe. This lent itself to an approach that searched for evidence and cause, a rule-based certainty. Psychoanalysis undoubtedly began its development along these lines, but theory was always modified by the recognition of individual differences and the uniqueness of each case. This has led more in the direction of a collection of truths rather than a single truth. Nevertheless, the concept of 'truth' has persisted.

Narrative therapy

In the 1980s and 1990s there was an explosion of interest in the 'narrative' therapies, an interest that McLeod (2003) links to the advent of post-modernism with its emphasis on deconstruction and the inadequacy of any grand or unified theory. In therapeutic terms all models focus to a degree on narrative – the client's account of their world, and the therapist's account of the client. McLeod's view is that narrative is not a therapy in itself but builds on existing schools, bringing a social constructionist view to bear on the individualistic nature of most therapies. White and Epson (1990), strong advocates of narrative therapy, originally came from the field of family therapy, already steeped in systems theory. Psychodynamic therapists also think in terms of systems, but internal ones, the object-relations world inside the mind of the individual.

Narrative therapy is interested in the stories that people have constructed in order to communicate what has happened to them. All therapies are interested in this, but for narrative work this is the main focus. One might say that a Freudian looks at stories through an Oedipal lens, a Kleinian through infantile phantasies, a Winnicottian through attachment, a Jungian through archetypes, and so on, so that to a degree all are 'narrative therapies'. But the strongest narrative therapy in the post-modern tradition is the social constructivist, which emphasizes the link between the individual and the social environment, to the degree that engagement with the social is a necessary component of therapeutic change: 'Personal identity is a product of the history of the culture, the position of the person in society and the linguistic resources available to the individual' (McLeod 2003: 234). Close attention is paid to the way in which a story is told: 'thinly', meaning from a narrow viewpoint, possibly self-blaming, uncontextualized; or 'thickly', resonant with many meanings and connections that enlarge both the narrative and the narrator. Vocabulary is important and gives clues to the world view that is behind the story. An individual can get caught in the mythology of their culture – rape is the woman's fault if she 'led the man on', unemployment is a special shame to a man, and so on. In therapy the narrative is placed outside of the individual into the area of relationship between self and society, and is reauthored using the normally cast-off parts of the story, the times when the client has been powerful, has impacted on their environment, encouraging them to locate their personhood equally in these successes as in the stories of failure. This positive approach has much in common with Rogerian therapy and some of the more solution-focused short-term work. The client is the expert, and is helped by the therapist to reauthor their own story. White and Epson (1990) elicit much of this change through questioning, but narrative therapy does not have to be word based; the work can equally be done through art or drama or music, and letters are often used to give the new story weight and concreteness.

Humanistic therapies

Understanding the way in which clients express or construct themselves through the use of language is an integral part of the theoretical underpinning of any clinical work (Russell, 1989). This is particularly so in the humanistic therapies where the importance of the dialogue between the client and the therapist is a fundamental part of developing a therapeutic relationship.

In Gestalt therapy, with its phenomenological emphasis and its orientation towards the client's process of self-discovery, exercises, confrontation and questions are used. The therapist is alert to the language of the client as an important source of information about how the client functions in their world outside the therapy room. For the Gestalt therapist the way in which a client speaks can signal for example learned helplessness, an underlying belief that they cannot help themselves, that they must remain stuck, or an intentionality, a positive capacity for action. Understanding these signals can help the therapist to have a better understanding of the individual. The contact of the organism, the inner person, with their external environment, is a central concept of Gestalt theory. It is at this point of interaction that blocks or difficulties in being can occur. These are called 'interruptions to contact' and five major ones have been identified – confluence, introjection, projection, retroflection and egotism (Clarkson 1999) – all of which are reflected in the way the client uses language.

Confluence represents a way of being where the individual seeks to be at one with the world in an attempt to merge their identity with their environment. It is reflected in language by the 'we's' that are frequently used by a person, suggesting that in *their* world everyone feels the same emotion, thinks the same thought or shares the same opinion. What is missing is the reality of the uniqueness of the individual. Someone who is overly confluent will use diffuse impersonal language to protect themselves from contact.

Introjection represents the attempt to internalize the demands of powerful characters that have populated the client's life. To say 'I should have' indicates living by adopted rules rather than creating an individual code, and introjective language is used to convince the client as well as those around them that they believe what they are saying.

Projection involves putting parts of the self out into the environment, disowning them and giving them to others. Rather than saying 'I know' or 'I feel', the client will say 'it seems' or 'there is', for example, 'there is anxiety within this team' instead of 'I feel anxious within this team'.

Retroflection is at the opposite end of the spectrum, when the client finds it difficult to put anything of themselves out into the environment. Someone who is retroflective will therefore be slow to talk and will struggle to make a point. 'This sounds stupid', 'I don't know', 'I'm not making myself clear', all reflect the internal struggle against silence, and silence itself may be the preferred option for a retroflective person. Counter-transferentially the therapist can then feel a desire to fill the silence with their own words and the predominant language of the therapy can easily start to belong to them.

The *egotistic* speaker will find speaking an end in itself, a chance to display their verbal ability rather than a focus on the substance of what they are saying. Long words and complicated sentences with little meaning hide the lack of a real engagement from the speaker.

Each of these orientations may be present in differing degrees in all people at various times and situations. One of the aims of Gestalt therapy is therefore to encourage the client to experiment verbally as a way of creating change in their interaction with the environment, for example using 'I' instead of 'one' or 'we' as an experiment in taking responsibility for or owning a feeling.

As shown earlier, the importance of what dreams tell us about ourselves has long been recognized (Freud 1900a/1953, 1900b/1953; Perls 1969; Jung 1978). Gestalt therapy views the dream as an existential message, and in this it is not unlike Jungian practice. The different parts of the dream represent fragments of the dreamer's personality. In working with the dream these fragments are put together to create a whole picture. Sleep becomes a screen upon which a film runs that projects disowned, unrecognized or repressed parts of the self. The dream is 'calling our attention to unfinished business' (Parlett 1993).

For example, Anne is a trainee psychotherapist and during the course of her training group with a Gestalt facilitator she presents a recurring dream. In it she is confronted by a large black rat. Its eyes are an opaque grey colour and she feels that it is very close to her, looking up at her as if about to bite her. However, the rat does not hurt her but instead smiles at her and touches her gently. What she recounts is remembering the fear of anticipating a sharp and painful bite and then the confusion of expecting one thing but actually experiencing something very different. Anne is encouraged to recount the dream in the present tense, and to explore what elements of the dream she might identify with. The energy in her recounting seems to lie with the image of the rat trapping her, not letting her go and she is encouraged to look at what this represents for her. Gradually Anne recognizes that the rat represents the challenge that the training group has presented her with over her introspection, her quietness within the group. The trapped feeling relates to the group's challenge to her retroflection – a favourite defence against contact. Her confusion is that this should hurt but it does not. Her unfinished business is to respond to this challenge in a non-defensive way. She also recognizes another part of her which does not want to run away from the 'rat', the group.

The Gestalt approach encourages clients to explore what parts of themselves are represented in dreams and whether they may be disowning these parts, unwilling to address them, or whether they may be able to create a whole picture through combining them differently.

The way in which Gestalt therapy uses language to understand the inner psyche helps us to understand how powerful language is. The notion of 'cognitive imperialism' (Mollon 2003) and verbal abuse as a form of bullying, combined with the inherent inability of language to do justice to our inner affect, make a potent weapon against those cherished goals of all modalities of therapy: self-awareness, self-fulfilment, choice and change. These concepts are explored further in Chapter 5.

In the person-centred approach the unconditional positive regard of the therapist for their client is one of the core conditions that underpins successful therapy. An essential element in this is understanding what has been described as the client's 'personal language' (Mearns and Thorne 1988: 64), or how they express themselves emotionally both through behaviour and verbally. This provides a holistic picture for the therapist in grasping the underlying meaning of the client's presentation. Other core conditions are congruence and empathy, and while these have been distinguished from the other through the way they are present in the person of the therapist (unconditional positive regard being an attitude, empathy a process and congruence a state of being), part of the essence of each is the language used by the therapist to communicate them.

The therapist encourages the client to symbolize their inner experiences for themselves rather than offering them interpretations. In a person-centred or client-centred approach the therapist endeavours to track moment by moment the client's processes so that the verbal responses of the practitioner are reflective and empathic, with the aim of facilitating the client to expand on their own perspective. Using a person-centred approach to explore Anne's earlier dream the therapist would be careful to allow Anne to gain awareness of what the dream meant, using attunement to identify her feelings and reflection to verbalize them. The therapist might reflect back to her a part of the dream: 'the way you describe the pain of a sharp bite feels very real and frightening'. This moves the story on a little without changing it as it gives Anne the chance to explore what she has said, moving into the reflexive frame (Forness-Bennett 1997).

The core concept of transactional analysis (TA) is that understanding the patterns of relationship between self and other will lead to increased understanding about the self and the self's response to others. 'Transactions' refers to interactions with both self and other. The style of communication, the most overt form of which is personal language, reflects the basic life position that the individual adopts as a child, which they then hold, consciously and unconsciously, throughout life (Berne 1964). An important tool for the TA therapist is their understanding of the client's language as indicative of their standpoint, the basic position from which they live their lives.

Cognitive-behavioural therapy

Cognitive-behavioural therapy (or CBT) uses language as a cognitive tool. It has its own vocabulary which is not generally shared with the humanistic and psychodynamic therapies – 'schemata', 'safety behaviours' and so on – but despite this it emphasizes the use of demystifying, accessible language in working with clients. Like narrative therapy CBT focuses on the client's story, but looking for the cognitive aspects, the way in which clients interpret their experiences, as it is in the interpretation that 'faulty' thinking can be detected. This is why one person's disaster is another person's challenge (Ellis 1962; Beck 1995). Grief for one person is a terrible, painful but natural process to be undergone; for another it is proof that they are bad, unlovable and that everybody will leave them.

   Because of the emphasis on cognition CBT is often portrayed as a rather cold affair, only responsive to one dimension of the client's experience. In fact emotions are taken to be very important as the goal of therapy is usually to *feel* better, not to think better. The point for CBT is that the one will lead to the other. The emotion is treated as a symptom and helping the client to change their thinking will prevent the negativity that reinforces the low feeling. The CBT therapist therefore pays close attention to what the client says. The words they use will give clues as to faulty thinking, or cognitive conceptualization. 'Shoulds', 'musts' and 'oughts' for example can indicate overly critical thinking, based on false expectations of life and the self. The client will be encouraged to describe things in their own words, to say exactly what it is they are feeling and thinking. This will be in a more structured way than in, say, person-centred therapy. The client may be asked to rate the level of their emotion on a scale of 1 to 10, or to fill in a depression or anxiety inventory. 'When do you generally feel worst? What specific thoughts or images go through your mind at that time? What have you done to cope with this in the past?' The precise phrasing used to describe core beliefs and resultant automatic thoughts is highly significant as it forms the basis of the therapy plan. The therapist will be at pains to ensure they have captured it properly, often writing down the words used during the session and checking in subsequent metings to see if the words have changed. This also helps to form the therapeutic relationship as the client experiences the therapist as genuinely interested in them and their views.

Images as well as words are important. Beck (1995) gives a case example of a depressed young college student whose thoughts moved quickly from academic struggles to failing the course to never making anything of herself, and this was accompanied by an image of herself walking alone down a street, homeless and desperate. In one image the cognitive distortion was exposed, which in this case was 'catastrophizing', or predicting the future at its most negative without including more likely, positive outcomes.

Socratic questioning – identifying unhelpful or irrational thoughts by asking questions that expose them through dialogue – is an important change agent in CBT. This assists clients to identify faulty thinking for themselves and is seen as much more effective than a didactic interaction, as it engages the client in the process of change. The emphasis is on opening up subject areas and clarifying implicit or explicit goals by means of the client's own discovery. Probing questions are often combined with reflections to this end (Wells 1997). It requires a very precise use of language by the therapist. The 'homework' may then be for the client to notice and write down how successful (or not) they have been at making the changes they agreed to try over the course of the week.

Homework is an integral part of CBT. The client will be encouraged to keep a log, write things down during the week, stay aware of their thoughts and how they influence feelings. Apart from the growing evidence for the therapeutic benefit of writing in its own right (Wright 2004), homework is seen to be part of the active engagement between therapist and client, and is planned collaboratively with constant reviews.

A danger of CBT is that its use of words becomes seen as simply clever or controlling. Padesky (1993) draws a clear line between changing minds and guiding discovery. The latter requires the therapist to be willing not to know in advance where they are heading, but to be working truly in collaboration with the client. The language is precise, but is most effective when attuned to the meanings given to it by the client.

Conclusion

Despite wide-ranging differences in the various therapies, common themes do emerge in relation to language. All therapies pay close attention to the client's communications, verbal and non-verbal. Words are a main agent of change whether this is from a cognitive standpoint that uses them as effective tools for thought or an analytic one that sees speech itself as a containing and modulating agent. Words are not just for talking *about* something; they are part of the experiencing of that thing as a recollection, so it *is* in the room by virtue of being spoken about. That is why clients are given time and space to reveal what they want to say. Speech connects the inner world to the outer one, and by putting something into words the client readies themselves for that connection. The therapist holds the safe environment in which words can be spoken, heard and responded to.

C H A P T E R   **4**

Communication without words:
another language?

Nicola Barden and Tina Williams

Theoretical approach and arts therapies

Art, understood broadly, is used by all therapeutic approaches, in a sense no differently from language. The thinking behind its use changes with theoretical orientation, yet there are surprising similarities. The artwork is assumed to hold meaning, and the meaning is thought to be potentially helpful. The therapist and the client collaborate to release possible meanings.

What follows is a brief summary of theoretical orientation and the therapeutic use of the arts, therapeutic techniques that in part relinquish the primacy of spoken language, which is psychotherapy's best-known medium. This is followed by a study of the relationship of language to the main arts therapies, and a consideration of language and consciousness, in particular through examining aspects of deaf history and sign language. Specific forms of specialist therapies are then observed to show how they relate communication to forms other than word alone.

Psychodynamic

In the strict Freudian interpretation art is a form of sublimation of the libido (Freud 1905/1953). This is typically read as a negation of its value by more humanistic practitioners for whom drive theory appears to reduce the human spirit to a mere collection of instincts. However, sublimation has a central role in enabling people to live controlled lives that can take others into account. It uses the energy of the initial drive or instinct to fuel an alternative and more complex expression of the life force, which in turn allows its transformation into a more consciously aware form (Kramer 2001). Art comes between instinct and discharge. Traditionally sublimation is viewed as a positive way of managing deprivation, as religious orders might transform the need for sex and family into a commitment to care and community; or as some artists have managed loss, through expression in music or painting. For the therapist, the artistic product or performance holds the meaning of the repressed thought or feeling, and offers an opportunity to bring it to consciousness. The artwork mediates between what is known and unknown by providing a symbolic communication; it can show what is not yet available to thought, yet is still expressible in a different medium. Not unlike a dream, art needs decoding, and psychodynamic arts therapies are no different from psychodynamic verbal therapies in that they seek to do this through paying attention to the transference. It is expected that the therapeutic relationship will contain, in addition to its own components, elements of the past which it gathers to itself through projections and identifications, so that it offers a blueprint of the past through the enactment of elements of it in the present.

Where there is difficulty in symbol formation art can help to develop the capacity to symbolize. The visual can be less frightening than the verbal (Wilson 2001) perhaps because it can be more opaque, and can better represent the uncertain, pre-conscious awareness that cannot yet find expression in the specificity of spoken language. Drama, art, music, all represent the internal world of the client, the collective and personal unconscious. Mediation between conscious and unconscious occurs continually in the mind through images, free association, fragmentary thoughts, remembered dreams; artwork facilitates this in a way that can be shared, or at least observed, by another, and so be brought into the realm of the therapeutic relationship. This comes back to the centrality of the transference in psychodynamic arts therapies.

There was always tension between Freud and Jung over Freud's view of psychotherapy as a scientific, medical-based discipline, and Jung's more arts-based approach (Rycroft 1985). Although Freud paid attention to dreams and images, he worked with them through words: 'Art can offer a spark in the "dark night of the soul", but analytic understanding mediates' (Schaverien 2001: 116). Jung valued the image itself as a natural form of expression for the psyche, and found the symbol effective in itself, not necessarily reliant on verbal translation. Jung's (1916/1976) transcendent function spoke to the heart of arts therapies, and Jung is often seen as particularly relevant to this field. As a boy he carved himself a little mannikin and stored it secretly in the attic of his house, checking it from time to time (Jung 1963). This seemed to reassure him and to contain some of his wordless anxieties. As an adult he would spend time sculpting, painting and drawing as a way of silently processing his emotional life. These activities required neither witness nor speech, but the activity itself gave opportunity for symbolic work which spoke directly of and to his needs. The transcendent function is precisely this, in that it mediates opposites by way of the symbol (Samuels et al. 1986). Jung saw it as a use of the energetic tension created by the very opposites it sought to mediate. Moving away from one-sidedness, art finds a way of holding the opposites in this creative energy that eventually resolves them. The symbol is the unifying factor. Art therapy focuses attention on the symbol, and on creativity (Jung 1931/1954). The client creates symbols as a route to resolution, trying to capture the essence of an unfinished experience or impulse in order to bring it to completion. Art reflects and transcends the experience and, exactly as Jung indicated, brings a new place into being.

Jung's valuing of artistic processes has placed him outside the mainstream psychodynamic field, but has endeared him to many humanistic practitioners; in a way he has creatively transcended the difference between the two approaches through his vision of the collective unconscious.

Humanistic

Humanistic practitioners tend to share an optimistic view of human nature, trusting that if natural forces are allowed to flourish then people will grow and develop in a positive way. Negative growth is seen as the result of poor environment, including the early nurturing relationship. People are not a bundle of potentially explosive drives that need taming, but essentially relational beings with an instinct towards the good, as long as that is not impinged upon. The focus is on creative potential, not illness, and the creative drive is a primary process, not a secondary structure (Garai 2001). The therapeutic relationship is therefore essentially benign; a nurturing environment which gives a corrective space. In that space the individual can express their fears and concerns in a safe and non-judgemental environment which allows for growth and does not get in the way of the client's work. The emphasis therefore is not on interpretation, and the idea of

the therapist as 'expert' is not relevant; but on collaborative exploration, with the client in control of the direction and content of the
session.

Because art images are understood as speaking most directly from
the unconscious, or an instinctual space that has not yet been brought
into thought, they are seen as deeply authentic, untrammelled by
the limits and expectations of the receiving environment, assuming
the counselling room to be a facilitative space. Whereas in psychodynamic work the image would normally be allowed to occur spon-
taneously and could therefore be interpreted as arising out of the
transference, in humanistic work there may be more structure, offering or suggesting image work around a theme recognized as being of
importance. Because the answers must come from the client the questions become more important – What does this image say to you?
If it was a colour, what would that be? What would that old man in
the drawing say if he could talk? Experience and feeling are central to
a humanist perspective. Artwork allows for buried feelings to be
brought into focus and fully experienced in a manageable way, initially through the mediating influence of the art. This will possibly be
with the help of a group to share the load, and with this connection
broken-off parts of the self can be brought back into awareness. If
psychodynamic art therapy is about insight, then the humanistic
process is about healing. It is not a route to diagnosis but a way for the
therapist to help the client be more fully in touch with their world.
For the client there are two stages to the work, that of creation, and
that of being empathically witnessed, and both are transformative.
For the counsellor 'using the arts as another language brings [them]
even closer to the client's world' (Rogers 2001: 165).

Gestalt, rooted as it is in existential philosophy and phenomen-
ology, concentrates even more on the here-and-now experience of
the client through artistic expression. The therapist's role may be
more fully as conductor, encouraging exploration of each role or note
or stroke made by the client, or making links across different media by
suggesting the client acts a particular drawing or plays a colour on an
instrument. The point is to fully inhabit each expression and so to
enlarge the self. Jung saw the self as an archetypal image of wholeness,
the initiator and goal of psychic life (Samuels et al. 1986), not entirely
benign, more amoral, but the sphere inside which the ego worked to
create a conscious response to the world. Humanistic practitioners
place more emphasis on the self as naturally positive if provided with
the right environment, and such provision is the healing task of the
therapist.

Psycho-educational approaches

These simply emphasize the learning/knowledge component of arts therapies. An educational approach has links to the whole occupational health aspect of arts therapies, and is particularly appropriate in the field of learning difficulties.

The behavioural approach concentrates on symptoms, and the therapist uses art-related techniques to help the client manipulate the symptoms so that they cease to be a problem. Roth (2001: 198) gives an example of a 6-year-old boy who was unable to paint a likeness of a house. This reflected a difficulty in comprehending the meaning of the objects around him, which had resulted in him setting fire to his home, apparently unable to associate meaningfully to the consequences of his action. The therapist's aim was that the boy should be able to draw a house in a recognizable form. This was achieved using guidance and reinforcement, until the boy made many forms of houses and eventually of other objects too, including people. This improved his conceptual awareness, and eventually he made a drawing of fire.

Cognitive-behavioural therapy built on the behavioural approach of the 1960s. This impacted on art therapy with a focus on the underlying thought patterns that could be revealed in images, as well as on the behavioural outcome. Art was seen as 'a concrete record of inner processes' (Rosal 2001: 217). Drawings could usefully accompany cognitive goals, for example being done before, during and after a planned programme of change. While recognizing spoken language as intrinsically related to cognitive skills, CBT acknowledges that the arts can develop parallel cognitive symbols. This is evidenced through an observation of sign language which integrates the linguistic and the iconic into a fluid whole.

The psycho-educational approach emphasizes the use of art in the service of learning. It is more structured than exploratory, focused on cognition and action rather than feeling and experience. It focuses on the external problem or symptom and has a corrective aim.

Words and language

Because language is ubiquitous and the majority of it is spoken, there is an expectation that 'language' means the spoken word; moreover, that language is what separates humans from animals, and that it is the medium of thought as well as communication. The corollary has also been accepted, that people who could not learn language were not fully human, and certainly had no access to thinking processes. Inheritance laws were only changed in sixteenth-century Spain because a nobleman, to prevent loss of property to his family, taught his deaf son to speak – so proving him to be human, and therefore able to inherit (Furth 1966). Although it has been a long time since such extreme prejudice has been part of society, it is relatively recently that other changes have been made, and the underlying prejudice is arguably not that far away. In order to examine communication without words it helps to examine language without the spoken word, and through this unpick what really is essential for a language to be a language, and a thought to be a thought.

Language and consciousness

A brief look at the history of deaf education in Europe is revealing about the western assumptive base regarding language and consciousness. There was a real question as to whether it was possible to think without language, it being believed that an inability to speak led to the development of lower intelligence. Language was seen as 'the gauge of human intelligence ... key to all that is abstract and conceptually mature in man' (Furth 1966: 3). Not until the second half of the twentieth century was it considered that it might be the coercive teaching of spoken rather than signed language that was responsible for the lower achievement rates in schools for deaf children. The 1880 Congress of Milan rejected the use of signing as a means of communication in schools and recommended the use of oral methods alone in deaf education. Under the Skinnerian influence of reinforcement, the repeated naming of objects and repeating of sentences in classes did not help deaf children to understand how a grammar was put together, particularly when they were discouraged from learning the language of sign that best matched their capacity for recognition and expression: 'The focus was on the development of speech, often to the detriment of language and almost always to the detriment of genuine education' (British Deaf Association 1992: 4). The intention was perhaps nobler than the act – full integration with the mainstream society – but it rested on the assumption that only a spoken language could achieve the subtlety and flexibility required to facilitate thought.

In the early 1900s, in accordance with the Milan Congress and reinforced by a Royal Commission Report in 1889, deaf teachers were replaced by hearing teachers, who could not sign at all until they were slowly trained to do so. The language of instruction was oral. This was akin to putting a native English speaker in a class full of Swiss speakers and expecting them to absorb the language through simply being surrounded by it. The actual result of such methods on their own is bafflement, demotivation and increased isolation (Abrams 2006). From the 1950s many of the schools were residential, starting a process that often continued into a segregated adult life until the 1978 Warnock Report (DES 1978) recommended integration into mainstream schools. Language development became stuck at the reading age, unlike for hearing children, so the deaf children had only the bluntest of instruments with which to express themselves and to understand the world around them. In this situation it is easy to see how poor language skills could be read as the cause of lower intelligence, with efforts to teach spoken language redoubled. But all the time this missed the sophistication and potential of the sign language that the children inevitably taught themselves and in which, once outside the classroom, they spoke to each other. 'Whatever the policies within the classroom, and whatever the rules about signing outside it, deaf children always seem to have managed to create opportunities to communicate using sign language' (British Deaf Association 1992: 5).

The first major study of sign language was published in America in the 1960s (Stokoe 1960), since which time studies have multiplied and sign has been truly appreciated as a language in its own right, and the first language of many deaf people. It is a living language, with its own dialect within a country and major differences between countries; American, British, French and Irish sign languages are all quite distinct from each other. As counselling is a rather new profession there are as yet relatively few standard signs for counselling concepts, for example the difference between 'listening' and 'active listening'; the meaning will be up to the signer to communicate, and will depend on their own familiarity with the concepts.

Sign itself is a combination of the iconic and linguistic aspects of communication (Kennedy 1995), reflecting the visual and oral expression of the child, the 'scribbling and babbling' that form the building blocks of language skills. Signing is a combination of a shape, made by the hands, the placement of the shape – the hands in relation to each other, to the rest of the body, to the listener – and movement, of hands and body in relation to each other. These elements are often directly symbolic and/or representational, unlike spoken language where the relationship between form and meaning is arbitrary. For example, Australian, American, British and Irish sign languages all have descriptions of 'cat' that can be related to a representation of whiskers, but each delivery of this representation is different (British Deaf Association 1992). Facial expressions are also a lively part of the communication, and words are mouthed to facilitate lip reading.

Sign language is by nature expressive: voice inflection and pacing are amply replaced by the combination of shape, placing and movement. Because the majority of deaf children are born to hearing parents, sign language is learnt at a later stage than usual for language acquisition. If both parents sign, then it is learnt as easily as a spoken language; in fact hearing children of deaf signing parents will also quickly become fluent in sign language.

Through his experiments with the out-of-sight object (see Chapter 1), Piaget and others determined that thought precedes speech: the object can be represented in the mind before there are words to describe it. Vygotsky (Butterworth and Grover 1988) pointed out that primates can solve problems that require thought, although they do not speak. This challenged the behaviourists' view of thought as a kind of 'silent language' (Furth 1966). With psycholinguistics emphasizing language as more than an expression of facts, the emphasis returned to the symbolic function of words, and language as an expression of thought rather than the means of it. Thus thought is essentially symbolic and independent of language, but uses language to give itself shape and form, and to bring itself into relationship with others.

Bodywork

Therapeutic bodywork is based not only on old practices of 'healing arts' – shiatsu, massage, tai chi and the like. It claims its presence in the beginnings of western psychotherapy, such as in the actions of Freud, who initially would place his hand on his patient's forehead to aid recollection of unconscious material. While Freud did not go any further down the road of touch with patients, his ego psychology was rooted in the body, and it was through the body that the most primitive drives and elementary stages of development were expressed. He saw the ego itself as sited in the body: 'The ego is first and foremost a bodily ego; it is not merely a surface entity, but is itself the projection of a surface' (Freud 1923/1995: 636–7). That is, the earliest experience of mediation between inner and outer is the surface of the skin, through which holding and abandonment, comfort and distress, become part of mental life and thereby the formation of the self. For Freud neurosis often came about because of the ego's failure to negotiate successfully between the id and the superego, that is, the drive to satisfy instinctual desires versus the prohibitions placed on such satisfaction by the requirements of 'civilization'. Many of his patients presented with somatic symptoms that were within the cultural expectations of the era – hysterical paralysis, headaches, attacks of pain, so that the body was literally an expression of the unconscious id. He treated these first with hypnosis and catharsis and then, as his theories developed, into understanding of the under-lying psychological conflict, bringing it into the light, making the unconscious conscious.

Freud (1925/1995) was fascinated by Darwin whom he felt held out 'hopes of an extraordinary advance in our understanding of the world' (p. 4). Darwin's evolutionary links between humans and pri-mates influenced Freud's (1913/1995) consideration of the incest taboo. While Freud worked to transform bodily feelings into verbal expression, others took Darwin's evolutionary observations as evi-dence of a sort of purity about physical communication that placed it above words, which unlike the body could misrepresent as well as attest. Lowen, a major contributor to the field of bioenergetics, quoted Darwin to this end: 'The movements of expression in the face and body . . . serve as the first means of communication between the mother and her infant. . . . They reveal the thoughts and intentions of others more truly than do words, which may be falsified' (Darwin 1872, cited in Lowen 1971: ix). This apparent divergence between a body therapy focused on expression and a talking therapy focused on interpretation is better understood when the roots of the former can be seen in the latter. Ferenczi (1953), a colleague of Freud's, noticed that relaxation aided free association and so linked the body with the storing of feelings: relax the body, and the feelings could surface and be brought to conscious awareness.

Reich (1927), the founding father of bioenergetics, was a pupil of Ferenczi's. He too found that the body manifested the dilemmas of the mind, but went further, saying that as the body 'remembered' the mind's unease, the act of freeing the trapped physical energy in the body in itself unlocked the mental anxiety; there was a truth to this physical communication that did not require and need not be fur-thered by verbal communication. This could be achieved through body therapy when normal physical discharge of energy was ham-pered through the somatisation of distress. Reich went further and suggested that illness itself was a result of repression and attributed

Freud's cancer to this cause – a theme that continues to be explored among some body therapists today while being sharply rebutted by others (Sontag 1991).

Analysis has always acknowledged the body as an alternative instrument to speech: 'psychoanalysis, following Freud, has privileged the role of language in the structuring of the psyche and in psychoanalytic treatment. But not all communications use language' (McDougall 1989: 11). Illness may be the best possible defence against overwhelming anxiety. However, the mind is seen by McDougall as *deprived* of its own experience when it is translated directly into the body. While the eloquence of the body's language is not doubted, it requires, in analytic theory at least, a more mentalised symbolic expression that is open to communication in the consulting room in order for it to be open to change.

These two positions, although they connect with one another, remain dichotomous in the practice of body therapy and indeed all the non-verbal therapies. Do arts therapies provide a means to reach language, or do they render language unnecessary? In a sense this question is only possible because of the mind/body duality referred to in Chapter 2, in which notions of consciousness are tied in with speech and language so that putting something into words is privileged as a higher consciousness. Yet libido in its earliest form *is* muscular energy. 'It would be wrong to speak of the "transfer" of physiological concepts to the psychic sphere, for what we have in mind is not an analogy but a real identity: the unity of psychic and somatic function' (Reich 1972: 340). Totton (2002a) questions how it is possible to fully and simultaneously inhabit the body and the mind, to 'breathe and relate' at the same time. His solution is for the therapist to work with the transference through the body. Working with the body is to work with the past in the here and now, if it is accepted that the body contains the physical traces of emotional trauma, and this brings the dichotomy into a unity. The formula offers a route for the energy-based work of Reich and the experiential approach of humanistic body therapists to connect back to their analytic origins.

However, post-Reichian therapy was more open to American than European influences. America was much more responsive to object relations within a humanistic framework, with the human core no longer a balance of drives and inhibitions but a life-seeking, self-regulating whole. The therapist was an equal partner and therapy a shared journey. There was a reaction against the therapist as 'interpreter' of the client's experience (though this is itself a questionable stereotype of much analytic work) and an emphasis on the client discovering their own meaning, with the therapist as a companion on the journey. In this way the therapist could engage directly with id processes, get involved at the level of one unconscious speaking to another, and there was no better container for this than bodywork. As interpretation was no longer central, nor verbal communication, body language could become the language of the therapist as well as the client. 'The body is both a representation and a reality . . . The body has a language with which it responds to life, and is itself a language constituted by the language it carries, which speaks through us and ultimately speaks us' (Gvirtzman 1990: 29).

The body could give information literally in musculature tension and metaphorically, for example a frozen shoulder as an introjection of being 'cold shouldered' by colleagues, numbness in the legs as 'not having a leg to stand on' (Carroll 2002). Responses to trauma may be stored in the body (Rothschild 2002), painfully embodied, for example in eating disorders and self-harm, as well as symptomatic illnesses. Therapists can get alongside and work directly with the body, using massage to release tension, and along with the release of tension activate the uncovering of memories and associations. The client can weep or rage or dance with no explanation required, simply going where their body takes them. This in itself is sufficient, partly as a catharsis but also because if the body is free of what it holds in, then it no longer stores the unconscious material. It has been let go. This does not require verbalization to make it real: 'If you want to help someone . . . turn the person inward towards experience. Don't turn them inward for explanations. Don't ask them why they feel that way – you're wrecking the process right there. You are taking the ship ashore. Don't ask for explanations. . . . You don't need to understand a thing' (Kurtz 1985/2002: ii–iii).

This approach is deeply challenging for the 'talking therapies'. Bodywork that uses metaphor, or sees the body as a route to shared understanding, is more easily integrated. Language can then be part of the process: what if the shoulder could speak, what would it say? What would it feel like to change posture? What is brought up if normally tense muscles are relaxed? What if habitual movements are exaggerated or checked? Touch in this approach is not a forbidden zone but another area for facilitating body awareness, providing a 'contact boundary' that can be explored safely in the room (Staunton 2002: 71) Attention is paid to the body as a communicator for the mind, and language is used to link the two together in consciousness.

Body psychotherapy today tends to be about adjustment, discharge or process (Totton 2002b). Adjustment sees the therapy as corrective, realigning the body and, by association, the mind. Discharge emphasizes the need for the safe space of the consulting room and the expression of held-in feelings. Process sees the client as the guide and the therapist as the companion on a mutual journey. Though specific to body therapy, these approaches could hold true in general for most of the non-verbal therapies which, as further examination shows, have much common ground in their achievements and their dilemmas.

Dance therapy

Dance therapy is a good example of the inevitable crossover within the non-verbal therapies, as well as between verbal and non-verbal. Dance itself is an embodiment of the transition between the literal and the symbolic. First developed in a therapeutic sense in the 1940s, it is based on a belief in the unity of mind and body, and on the conviction that words alone are not sufficient to give expression to the human condition. It rests on another conviction that it is full expression that facilitates change. 'The dance therapist places special emphasis on encouraging dramatic movement metaphors that express the hidden and symbolic aspects of the self' (Levy 1995a: 3). Torment, for example, can be portrayed in the twist of a body (Bernstein 1995), which enacts the direct physical expression of the emotion while, by virtue of being an act, creating distance from it. This distance between the experience and the re-enactment is what allows for transformation through creative play. Torment can be consciously owned, given shape and allowed to transform. By being externalized it becomes available for reflection and thought, which may or may not be spoken.

Dance therapy can take place singly or in a group, and the therapist may act as conductor or interpreter. This will often depend on theoretical orientation, with more analytically minded dance therapists using body movements as a basis for comment on what the movements represent, and more person-centred/integrative therapists interacting directly with the client. In both approaches, at the point of dance the words are secondary to, or act in service of, the movement. Where in words the counsellor might ask, 'Can you say a little more about that?', the dance therapist might suggest a new movement to follow on from an existing one, or the exaggeration of one action to see where it leads, or bringing in another group member to do a mirroring dance so the client can see for themselves what is being portrayed. The therapist might dance with the client, in an improvised duet or simply alongside with eyes shut, to encourage and give permission, as well as to think together afterwards about how the two dances may have been 'speaking' to each other. In the same way an art therapist might paint alongside their client, or as part of a group. As in body therapy, new movement in itself can be seen as indicative of underlying psychological change, without the need for the symbolic dance to have verbal interpretation, or it can be seen as a basis for insight through talking about the movement, how it feels, why it was made, what it means. Either way the dance is the basis for the thought, whether conscious or unconscious. This way of working, where the expression of thought is not necessary, can be particularly helpful for work with children, for whom the experience of the moment is what counts (Levy 1995b). A child can create and enact a dance to 'get the bugs out' (Harvey 1995: 178) and use it repeatedly outside the therapy room to get rid of fearful associations, without having to understand why it works. Harvey's example of a child traumatized by sexual abuse illustrates how the dance itself expresses the feelings that need containment, the dance being understood as metaphor and responded to in kind, without the need for verbal detail that would be overwhelming at that stage. The safety and acceptance in the response offers a secure environment in which attachment needs can be experienced and met, thereby perhaps building up the ego conditions for more precise disclosure in the future. Fried (1995) goes further in describing work with a blind child with little developed concept of the 'other', who slowly engages in body/dance therapy: 'Jon relates through his body and the modality of movement; it is his natural language' (p. 163).

Where dance is more fully partnered with verbal language the therapist will interpret the metaphor (Rose 1995), using knowledge of the past to interpret the meaning of the present (Lavender and Sobelman 1995). Words may become part of the ritual or enactment through chanting, singing, linking voice with movement, using the group as a chorus, even asking the client to create a poem for the images they have just danced and then to recite the poem to the group (Bernstein 1995). It can liberate people of any age for whom words are not the best first language, people who need to show rather than tell, but to show in a way that facilitates communication and understanding at the level of metaphor. Most ballets are silent, but the story is eloquently told.

Drama therapy

Although often thought of as relatively new, drama therapy in fact has a long history extending back to its origins as a remedial or occupational therapy for inpatients in psychiatric institutions. Asylums like Broadmoor built theatres as early as the 1850s, and a programme from the Royal Bethlehem Hospital illustrates a staff performance of 'Ali Baba' given in the hospital's own theatre in 1897 (Allderidge 1997). This was part of a swathe of arts-based activities intended to provide patients with worthwhile occupation; the plays would often have a moral tone, and in its own way the theatre movement in hospitals is not unlinked to the Theatre in Education movement of the 1980s, taking theatre into classrooms to stimulate moral discussion and learning. Even though it was on one level entertainment, it also enabled personal dilemmas to be acted out on stage and brought into the collective, and thus be both recognized and contained. This is still the effect of good plays today, and has been the function of fairy tales and myths from time immemorial (von Franz 1970; Bettelheim 1976): 'It is possible to hold rehearsals, to try our strengths in a make-believe big world. And that is Play' (Cook 1917, quoted in Jones 1996: 67). Hospitals now seldom have their own theatres, but drama therapy is widely used by therapists in a similar spirit of providing a stage on which fears and anxieties can be externalized and transformed.

Drama as psychotherapy (psychodrama) was spearheaded by Moreno (1946), originally in Europe and then America. The play was no longer the thing, but the playing, in a structured way and usually in a group. Moreno emphasized the individual's self-healing capacity given the right environment. The activity itself was the therapy, not a vehicle for raising things in one-to-one work later on. A pattern emerged which consisted of a warm-up, an enactment, and a debrief. The therapist took the role of director and producer overall, though each client might direct their own individual drama, with guidance from the therapist. Holmes (1991) gives examples of typical classical techniques:

- Role reversal – the client/protagonist plays the 'other': father, sister, boss
- Doubling – a group member, elected as the 'auxiliary ego', doubles with the protagonist, offering unexpressed thoughts and feelings
- Surplus reality – enacting what cannot or has not happened
- Mirroring – the protagonist observes another person enacting their role

- Closure – revisiting the original scene and seeing if the psycho-drama has changed the experience for the protagonist.

Other group members are an important part of the cast. While no one need be expert in the dramatic medium, the therapist must be comfortable with both technique and inspiration, flexible enough to follow the client's needs and skilled enough to facilitate drama in the service of them. The client might, for example, improvise on a real trauma, work around a symbol remembered in a dream, play with props and see what emerges, or direct a group sculpture representing the family (Jones 1996). Jones emphasizes that drama is a way of participating in the world, not of mimicking it. This, like dance, emphasizes the capacity of the performance to allow for the externalization of projections, making them accessible to conscious engagement and change.

Since the 1980s drama therapy has been accepted in most theoretical orientations. It is not a therapy without words, as the actors may speak and the piece may be discussed afterwards. But, as is a theme in the arts therapies, it captures something that is not fully expressible in words alone, and that can only be symbolized: 'The symbol says that there is something it could say, but this something cannot definitely be spelled out once and for all; otherwise the symbol would stop saying it' (Eco 1984: 161). The body, the props, the words and movement, all combine in drama to give life to the symbol in a way that the drama therapist believes is beyond words.

Art therapy

Art therapy began to establish itself in hospitals after the Second World War as part of the effort to support and treat returning soldiers. The need to respond to traumatized, sometimes psychotic service personnel facilitated a period of creativity in the therapeutic world. Group therapy and therapeutic communities based in hospitals particularly benefited at this time as psychiatrists tried to offer something new to the people in their care (Foulkes 1964; Bion 1967). Perhaps because of the client group, treatment was closely allied to concepts of rehabilitation, and early art therapy was generally seen as something to keep patients occupied in a positive way, as being containing and productive rather than directly therapeutic. Practitioners often came more from an art education than a psychotherapy background. The world of art also underwent a transformative period around this time, perhaps in response to the upheaval and chaos of war. There was a move away from more directly representational art towards expressionism, and this coincided happily with the exploration of the inner/outer boundary that was the focus of art therapy.

As well as working with trauma, art therapists engaged with psychotic patients who were not expected to be responsive to more word-based therapies. Again, this coincided with the development of more radical therapeutic hospital communities in the post-war period, which gradually included art in their repertoire of interventions (Cole 1976), and more gradually included people with psychosis, not so much inside the communities as within the psychiatric wards nearby.

Art therapists developed a particular insistence that all states of mind could be worked with, perhaps because the nature of artwork is precisely to engage with the irrational and unconscious aspects of the self; and that all people, including those suffering from great disturbance, can and do make art (Barnes and Berke 1973).

> The drawings were presented to me by a very ill man who had been on a locked ward in the hospital for years. He was incontinent and unable to speak clearly. He had drawn vigorously on the only paper he could find [lavatory paper]. The top is filled with strange shapes and words which had a special meaning for him. The second strip depicted a lion and its mate, which he loved to draw repeatedly when he later came to the studio . . .
>
> (Adamson 1984: 9)

The 1960s and 1970s saw the gradual build-up of the anti-psychiatry movement (Laing 1959; Goffman 1961; Berke et al. 1995) finding new neighbours in the emerging professions of humanistic and existential therapy (Wood 1997) and the increasing popularity, and thus accessibility, of psychoanalysis (Waller 1991). Art had an equalizing effect: the point was not skill or erudition but a simple rendering of the self through a means that could be apprehended if not always understood. Art therapists approached patients with genuine interest in their work and a level of artistic communication was within everyone's grasp.

As therapy itself became more professionalized in the 1980s and 1990s, art therapists became more firmly attached to the psychotherapeutic rather than the educative tradition, concentrating on models of intervention over the more general provision of a safe expressive environment. Theoretical underpinnings and technique were the focus, and with this there was once again a close alignment with the various underpinning therapeutic traditions (Wood 1997).

Perhaps more than other arts-based therapies art therapy itself allows the creation of a personal statement that may not be designed as a communication. It requires neither companion nor audience, though it may invite both. It can be done as a solitary activity even when in the presence of another and, when shared, lacks the element of performance. Art can engage with the object rather than with the creator (Jennings and Minde 1993). It remains itself after it has been created, unlike a performance which must be created anew each time. Both process and outcome are significant. Art is uniquely suitable for work with psychotic patients in hospital settings and can be effective in conditions where there is as yet little conscious understanding between therapist and client.

The environment of the art room is extremely important as it is an embodiment of the therapist and the therapeutic process. It can be used as part of the therapy, without needing words. Skailes (1997) describes a long-term patient who had spent 30 years living in institutions. His paintings were 'monochrome and featureless' (p. 206). Rather than interpret, Skailes injected life into the surroundings by bringing plants, flowers and stuffed animals into the art room. The patient focused on the animals and slowly created an environment for them in his paintings, using his imagination to provide contrast and background. Eventually he drew pictures of his own childhood and family. This work was not about facilitating a shared understanding of the pictures but about the therapist using her understanding of them to respond in a direct fashion that returned a sense of agency, and thus of self, to the patient. The therapist of course thought about what was being shown to her, and understood that the client could not take in a response that required engagement with the external world.

Schaverien (1997) describes this as a fetishistic use of art by the patient. It is pre-Oedipal and almost pre-relational, the artist relating only to their art because they are not yet able to take in the therapist or yet to receive another person's thoughts. The picture is constructed to bypass thought, and is influential but not relational – response is irrelevant. The parallel is with early infancy where the carer must supply the infant's needs as if they are not separate, and interruptions to the chain of demand and supply must be introduced gradually and carefully. Words for the infant and the client are not yet present for use as symbols, but a picture can grow that performs that role, once it has been invested with aspects of the self. In this way it can take on a meaning: 'In the juxtaposition of word and image, there is in the first place an attempt to fix the experience and communicate with the self, and in the second an attempt to communicate with the Other' (Schaverien 1997: 13).

The actual picture, therefore, whatever its contents, is a significant object in the therapeutic process, as is the artistic space itself (Wood 1997). Clients may want to throw pictures away but generally they are held till the work is completed, as a statement of value for the client and as an affirmation of the reparative potential that continues to exist. Because, as illustrated earlier, symbolism can be responded to without needing to acknowledge that it exists, it provides a strong safety factor for clients who can bear very little otherness. Art therapies are often seen as creative play in the Winnicottian (1991) sense, but the play may be solitary before it is shared. Sometimes the therapist may simply be in the same room painting alongside the patient and independently of them, later moving into joint consideration of the paintings side by side. Lachman-Chapin (2001: 73–5) gives an example: the client was painting a fish swallowing a hook that will bring down the boat; while the counsellor drew a nest of hungry hatchlings. Taking the two together prompted a discussion about the hatchlings' need to ruthlessly devour in order to ensure they stayed alive, and the fear that such hunger or need will overwhelm and drown the carer once they are hooked into the caring role. The pictures here were not fetishistic objects, even though they were constructed independently, because they were able to be used in relationship, in mutual play and creativity.

These examples demonstrate the capacity of art to speak from the unconscious in a relatively spontaneous fashion. The full meaning of the communication remains on canvas to be seen over time, and even to be heard in silence if that is what the client can manage. It is uniquely containing, in that the message and the medium can be infinitely manipulated. Some paintings will be revelatory, others will change in tiny ways over long periods. All can embody unbearable feeling, or give form to split-off parts of the self that are not yet ready for integration but may be open to consideration. Schaverien (1987) likens this to the picture as 'scapegoat', carrying the sins of the people into the wilderness. The art provides both disguise and message. She gives the example of a picture made of a transparent weeping figure attacked by arrows, covered by disjointed red lines. It was a communication to the person outside the painter of the painter's internal state. The picture carried and held that state, but allowed it to be shared with another. 'It reveals the pain of the potential fragmentation of psychosis in a way which no words could convey. There are times when words can add nothing to an image: the picture says it all – it is its own vivid and powerful interpretation' (Schaverien 1997: 29).

Of course not all art therapy needs to be covert. It can be a tremendous relief to find an expressive image that can be shared and have an impact on someone else, especially when the experience to be conveyed seems beyond words. Artwork can represent both inner and outer worlds, subject and object, in fact the philosophical approaches described in Chapter 2 make it impossible to disconnect them both – the artist always uses her or his own body to paint. The artwork becomes a 'symbolic language' (Jennings and Minde 1993: 48) to which the art therapist can respond. While most people can respond to art, the therapist's own facility in artwork is important because it enables the therapist to think more about the nature of what the client has created – the materials chosen, how they have been used, colour and light, and texture. This is combined with the therapist's psychological knowledge towards understanding the artistic expression of the client, and through this to find transformative potential. Use of three-dimensional art for example can bring about more primitive responses. A medium such as clay with its fleshly consistency can easily receive projections of hate and rage that would have been linked to the mother's body. Foster (1997) notes that patients often flatten plasticine into pancake shapes, as if to squash this fleshiness out of it and so avoid the projections. Making these phantasies conscious can ease the anxiety behind them and allow them room to develop into something else. As with other arts therapies, talking about the art may at some point be a crucial stage in the process as it allows for thoughts to be shared in a way that is conscious and can be continued in awareness outside of the therapy room.

Music therapy

The artistic spark in any setting can set things going: 'a sentence is a thing (noun) enlivened (verb); a tune is a string of sounds animated by rhythm. Familiarity with this process of "animation" may help to enliven the individual for whom the symbols of life have become stuck, including that of oneself as a cipher' (Yon 1993: 107).

Music therapy sustained a strong period of development in the 1980s and 1990s, although the earliest training in the United Kingdom was established in 1968. Although all arts therapies include work with children, music therapists in particular work with preschool and primary children, with adults with learning, emotional and behavioural difficulties and with adults exhibiting challenging behaviours.

Music is universally related to by very young children and used by parents as they instinctively sing, croon or use their tone of voice when communicating with infants. In the womb the foetus is constantly in the presence of the rhythm of the mother's heartbeat as well as its own, and external sound carries into the uterus, which is actually quite a noisy place. Music for adults has often been described as a universal language, and it crosses continents remarkably well. Music grows much like a language, as its influences combine and split apart to create something that is ever changing.

Although true to an extent of all arts therapies, music in particular lends itself to the interchangeability of affect, or 'affect attunement' to which babies can respond so well (Stern 2000). A facial expression can be mirrored through a tone of voice. One type of sound, like a crashing saucepan, can be moderated by another, for example a surprised 'ooh!' accompanied by raised eyebrows and an extra cuddle. In this way, sight, sound and touch come together as a coherent language to impart recognition, affirmation and reassurance, all at a pre-verbal stage.

In the same way that music can be used to moderate affect it can be used for expression of the same, and even very young children can improvise with drums, cymbals, triangles, as they can through rudimentary paintings and simple dances. Although the client need not have musical ability the therapist does need to be comfortable and have some facility in the field, as they must often supply the 'harmonic support' to hold a piece together (Bunt and Hoskyns 2002: 30), give it some narrative, and respond in a musical conversation. This enables the therapy to be conducted without words when necessary, and with a sort of indirect communication which can feel safer to a client for whom the 'other' is a shaky or untrustworthy concept. One mother commented of her child's experience, 'Music therapy was the perfect vehicle for a child with no language and little social awareness' (Bunt 2002a: 82). The therapist paces any intervention to the needs of the client. The idea of 'conversation' can be explored through duets, which can be harmonious or competitive. The therapist can sing a commentary on the client's actions, musically reflecting the client's rhythmic statements, and so on. The client can accept, ignore or reject these interventions, and so the work is done through a sort of musical dance.

Musical improvisation is analogous to spontaneous conversation, and is the core of music therapy (Sloboda and Bolton 2002). As with conversation the important thing is not the 'grammar' of correct play but the overall rhythm and pace and melody. Therapy takes place through the music so although the therapist will have their own understanding of the way the client's material is represented in the music, they are likely to respond musically rather than verbally. As with the other arts therapies there may be a verbal debrief afterwards.

Music and words can be combined so that a rhythm is established which a child, or a group, can shout out to, or a song can be made up so that the words made into a tune can address a particular anxiety (for example the monster under the bed). Moving something into a different medium emphasizes the capacity for transformation. The music comes between the emotion and the client and allows anxiety to be manipulated and played with in a way that can ultimately place the client in a different relationship to it. The music therapist can also act as a representative of the damaging/frightening/bewildering 'other'. Thus working with music can include working with the transference, only from the inside rather than as an observer/commentator role alone. 'Musical transformation can be a metaphor of psychological transformation' (Bunt 2002b: 293).

Conclusion

All animals communicate, but people are unique in the range of communicative possibilities open to them. Even the human face is structured differently to most other animals. It has muscles whose purpose appears to be solely to convey expression. Rather than being anchored to bone, facial muscles are anchored to each other in a complex network, and this enables them to move without affecting the skeleton. A smile is not a practical function – it does not enable eating or running or looking; it is primarily communicative. Expression can be controlled – the face can be a mask, not true to its owner. Infants can control the face in a way they cannot control other muscles. In part this capacity for facial expression is a result of evolution. The head is less important in catching food, does not need so many mechanical parts in working order; the eyes face forward so there is a broader canvas. Primates are most similar to humans in this and share a level of facial expression.

Caroline Garland, an experimental psychologist who initially studied chimpanzees, later trained as a psychoanalyst. She concluded that to understand anything beyond general social display in primates there has to be an amount of subjectivity in reading facial communication – the observer has to know the individual being observed, and understand what a movement means to *them*. 'There is no conceptual information which can be transmitted without language, but there is a lot of emotional language which can be' (Cole 1998: 69–70). Faces are unique, and crude guides on how to read body language come nowhere near meeting what a glance means to a particular person. Donna Williams, an autistic author, described in an interview with Cole how looking at someone's face could provide a simply overwhelming amount of information, comparable to having to take in a second language.

Infants are wired to respond to faces. Many studies show that they can identify facial expressions, that they prefer to look at faces and that they can identify the mother's face from others (Bushnell et al. 1989; Stern 2000). Cole (1998) sees facial movements mediating between the mind and the body, prior to the acquisition of language. Even where language is available, if facial expression is impaired, through illness or accident, communication suffers. The listener receives no visual feedback and as a result offers less engagement, establishing a negative feedback loop. Jokes are not laughed at, smiles are not returned. The speaker can manage the content of speech but not its affect and so is cut off from themselves as well as their listener: 'It seems very likely that losing facial animation meant not only losing expression and communication with others but led to a reduced intensity and delineation of feeling within oneself' (p. 150). It is a truism that the verbal element is of the smallest significance in communication (Mehrabian 1969), but one well illustrated by the loss of self that can accompany loss of congruent facial expression.

Arts therapies challenge the primacy accorded to language in the talking therapies. Words are powerful without doubt, and are conceptually necessary. Yet arts therapies offer a challenge that highlights the limitations of the spoken language. Speech is not the only container, nor even the best one. The therapist must be attuned to the person in order to understand them, whatever the mode of communication; and it may be that some things, within an attuned relationship, are as well or better expressed through the arts than they are through language. Of course there is no absolute divide between art and language any more than there is between the mind and the body. Nevertheless it is important to be reminded that all theoretical orientations include the arts in their repertoire, to a greater or lesser degree. The purpose is seen differently, as is the method of engagement, but the efficacy of their communication is universal.

Being with the other: the role of language in therapy

Tina Williams

The practice of psychotherapy, where two or more people sit together and talk, can be seen as a conversation – a reciprocal conversation, or dialogue (from Wikipedia.com). It follows from this that the therapy takes place through what is conveyed by the words used by each of the people in the conversation. However, the importance of words in the dialogue of therapy is not necessarily considered to be central by the practitioners of all modalities, who argue that dialogue can take place in different ways.

Dialogic therapy (Buber 1967; Hycner 1991) defines different types or concepts of dialogue. Among these are technical dialogue, mono-logue and genuine dialogue. The last of these, genuine dialogue, is more concerned with the openness of the interaction between people than the words used. This openness is a real desire to be with the other person and does not have to involve words at all – it can be silent. In contrast, technical dialogue is an objective exercise in getting infor-mation. Focusing on the content, it is very much concerned with words as the conveyers of information. The third type of dialogue is a monologue, a dialogue in disguise, because the spirit of truly wanting to interact with another person is missing. Instead the concern is with self, with no desire to understand or learn about the other. It is a monologue because the only voice that is heard is the speaker's own. Buber (1958) related these different types of dialogue to his concepts of I–Thou and I–It. Genuine dialogue is representative of an I–Thou attitude to relationship because it both values the difference of the other and also wants to know about that difference. This comes from an authentic desire to learn about the other person, to understand them and to join with them or meet them in relationship. The focus on self in the monologue and in the technical dialogue has the qualities of an I–It relationship. The other person is not seen or valued in their own right as another individual but is related to more as an object which can be used in the service of the self. The person using this kind of dialogue is not motivated by the intention to have a mutual relationship with the other, but rather by the desire to hear themselves more clearly, ignoring the other if necessary.

These different types of dialogue could be seen as aspects of fundamentally the same process. Communication has different functions: to gain information, to be heard and sometimes to experience mutuality, where there is enough emotional space for more than one person. All these aspects of dialogue use words to a greater or lesser extent and all can be seen in therapy. Some of these themes are taken up later in a more detailed examination of the therapeutic relationship.

The power of words

Words are symbols. They communicate in symbolic form how the world is perceived and construed. Those who name have power over those to whom names are applied. In the Judaeo-Christian creation myth, for example, when God gave Adam power over the animals this meant that he could name them (NEB Genesis 2:19).

Labels attach identities which represent the individual's place in the world (Heath 2002). This identity belongs to the individual whether they want it or not and whether or not it feels authentic. Once given it is difficult to change. 'The earliest cauldron for the manufacture and imposition of identity (is) the family' (Mollon 2003: 227), for example in the descriptions – quickly becoming labels – that may be applied to children: stupid, clever, noisy, quiet, selfish, kind, thoughtless, thoughtful, failure, success, beautiful, ugly.

Therapists similarly label clients. Diagnostic criteria such as those contained in the American Psychiatric Association (AAA) *Diagnostic Manual* (2000) and the European equivalent, the *International Classification of Diseases* (WHO 2003), give labels for a whole range of mental health conditions: obsessive compulsive, dependent, anxious, borderline. Therapeutic arguments against diagnosing point to the negative potential of labelling as the terms can become shorthand for describing the whole person instead of just one aspect of them. Therapeutic arguments in favour point to its uses, for example in facilitating a common understanding between practitioners about a person who may be at risk or who may be a risk to others.

The language of counselling and therapy has been cited as one of the elements that contribute to the inherent inequality in therapeutic process. One person is identified as having a problem: 'over-anxious', 'dependent personality', 'low self-esteem', while the other person is not. Gergen (1990: 210) powerfully describes this as an 'invitation to infirmity'. The term 'client' itself has been criticized for similar reasons, indicating a passivity in relationship to a professional (the therapist) who is doing something *for* them. The power of language is such that these names can impact on the dynamics of the relationship before it has even begun.

Identities even when imposed can be all too easy to adopt. Making it true for the individual, rather than trying to fight it, is at least a way of having some sense of ownership and control. Part of this 'making it true' process is to develop the identity further, building a personality around it. In this way language can be both empowering and dis-empowering (Heath 2002; Mollon 2003). Language, or naming, has the power to define what is normal and abnormal and it can be inclusive and exclusive. There are many examples of derisive terms used to describe individuals, groups, cultures and countries (Goffman 1961). Names can serve to impose the prejudices and fears of one group on another and to exclude those who do not belong to the dominant group. At the same time, this connects the dominant group more closely.

The psychological importance of our need to belong, to be part of a social as well as family group, was identified by Maslow in the 1940s. His hierarchy of needs (Maslow 1987) identified the key requirements necessary to facilitate the drive towards personal fulfilment. The five levels of need comprised: basic physical necessities such as food, drink and warmth; safety needs such as protection from the elements and law and order; belonging and love which included having a work group, family, affection and relationships; esteem including self-esteem and independence; and finally self-actualization, which included self-fulfilment and personal growth. Only when the lower order of requirements were met could higher order needs be addressed so that individuals could lead healthy and fulfilling lives.

Adolescents are masters at using words to define a sense of belonging: 'chavs', 'skaters', 'townies', 'geeks' are just a few examples of how a whole string of characteristics, from how someone dresses to the way they spend their leisure time, how they deal with authority to how much school work they do, can be summed up in one, labelling, word. No need for further explanation, no need to know the person – enough is known for them to fit in to a particular place in the world. It is a convenient word, a shorthand which means that someone can be described without being known. This also, however, has an important role in developmental growth for the adolescent. It offers a way of defining their world in order to define themselves in relation to that world. On a wider scale it is a reflection of the natural human instinct to form groups and allegiances, to belong to a system and to have common features rather than to be alone or unique.

In summary, standing out from the perceived norm by exhibiting any characteristic different to the majority, whether it be sexuality or size, physical or mental abilities, will result in labelling. Mollon (2003: 226) refers to this as 'cognitive imperialism', a form of aggression or verbal bullying, because the labels given are judgemental. '*The limits of my language* mean the limits of my world' (Wittgenstein 1922/1963: 115).

Chapter 2 on the philosophy of language has shown how experience of the world is structured through words. Words are 'the background against which we see any action' (Wittgenstein 1922/1963). They are subjective, judgement laden and culturally embedded. Given this, it is clear that the way we use language as therapists may not provide clients with enough space to find their own language and can easily repeat the family 'naming' experience (Clarkson 2001).

Finding an authentic voice is empowering; not having a voice as a way of making a mark, a name, is disempowering. Having the power to name reality, when it is handed to or appropriated by someone else, is at best frustrating and at worst takes away the capacity for self-fulfilment and actualization: it requires 'fitting in' rather than true belonging. Both the process of naming and the use of a predominant cultural language are expressions of power and both of these are found in therapy. Given that therapy is about the empowerment of the individual, it is not difficult to see how the goals of therapy can become distorted if attention is not paid to the issue of language. Mollon (2003) equates equality of opportunity with equality of power and that in turn equates to the opportunity to name the world. This is reflected in the predominance of western therapeutic models, which should not be seen as the only way of understanding the world. Heath (2002) issues a challenge to 'deconstruct these theories in order to allow them to become more porous to alternative ways of constructing the world and of the mind' (p. 45).

Everyone needs to have their own voice within a common language, to use language in their own way – which means being open to words having different meanings, to concepts not being the same for everyone. Being able to not just tolerate difference, literally paying lip-service to it but to actually recognize the importance and validity of, and strive towards, understanding individuality of meaning.

Developmental themes

In the same way that a child may have been forced to use their parents' language (either symbolically or literally) as they were growing up, the therapist can re-enact this potential source of difficulty for the client by imposing their own language which equally may not fit or belong to them (Totton 2004). One of the consequences of not paying attention to the role of language in therapy is that the therapist can re-enact the clients' early traumatic experience of being misunderstood or not heard at all. Perhaps the best that can be hoped for is an awareness of the relationship with language that parallels the therapist's awareness of relationships with people. In order to do this it is necessary to explore developmental patterns and the way that language can impact on them.

Stern (2000) focuses on the development of a sense of self through four phases, the fourth being a sense of verbal self during the infant's second year. During this stage the toddler begins to develop the capacity to use words themselves. The infant is no longer a wordless participant in the dialogue between himself and the external world. With misunderstanding being an inherent part of any communication with another, this phase of development can be the source of many difficulties later in life because of its impact on the sense of self. Stern sees all the phases of development as interlocking, impacting on each other, colouring the future developmental patterns and through this having an influential role in shaping the adult. Like a set of Russian dolls each of these phases fits inside the other, shaping and determining both the strength and weakness of the whole. The fact that Stern identifies the learning of a language, the verbal phase, as an integral part of the childhood development in the same way as other essential developmental phases of the sense of self such as inter-subjectivity and the development of a core identity is an indication of the fundamental importance of the child's relationship with language. Development in this verbal stage determines the future relationship with language and through this with the world later in life. Confidence in communicating clearly, or anxieties about appearing foolish or vulnerable when speaking, may all be themes that start when very young and lead to adult patterns ranging from verbosity to silence.

Inter-subjectivity, or the 'finding of self in recognition by and of the other' (Mollon 2003: 111), is crucial in self-development. It has positive and negative aspects, and in this the image of the mirror is relevant. The mirror is a metaphor for explaining how the infant is shown a picture of herself by the responses of those closest to her. These responses are often laden with the needs of the other person. The mirror is, so to speak, distorted and the picture that the child receives of herself is not always true. Language forms part of this mirror, part of the reflection that the child sees; it is this that is so influential in the subsequent identity that the child takes for herself.

Bollas's (1987) concept of the 'unthought known' is a way of describing an experience that has not been psychologically processed. An event that is out of the normal range of our day-to-day experience, for example bereavement, needs somehow to be understood and integrated, placed in the context of our previous experience and current understanding of the world. Using a metaphor here might be a good way of explaining the purpose of this. If a piece of mercury is loose then it is unpredictable, difficult to grasp and dangerous. Until it is contained it cannot be controlled, which results in anxiety – how dangerous is it? Will it affect everything it touches? This anxiety affects the rest of life making it very difficult to be attentive to anything else. The metaphor suggests life might be pointless or anxiety ridden if its different elements are not properly contained.

However, once contained, even if mercury remains a potent and dangerous liquid it is now under control. Thus it can be examined, experimented with and discovered for its positive as well as negative qualities. It can be left behind, or taken on into the future. Historically, events early in development that occurred before there were words to explain them can remain uncontained, having an impact without conscious knowledge of them. Words can help to contain experience by processing it. By being able to describe something, share it with another and have it affirmed and offered a different perspective, the experience can become understood and integrated. Putting words to events that have been a part of experience but were not spoken of before is an important aspect of therapy and the role of language within it.

In developing his theory of a personal construct system Kelly (cited in Bannister and Fransella 1971) envisaged how past experiences are used to form ideas of the world, to make hypotheses which are then applied to new situations. The purpose of these constructs is to understand past events and to interpret current and future ones. In order to function successfully constructs need to be flexible enough to accommodate new material and then to contract again. They can then reform into a new structure of ideas that continue to be predictive. It seems a natural conclusion that the way language is used and the choice of words are a reflection of an underlying system of individual personal constructs. If therapists are to have a new way of using language based on client experiences, then one way of understanding the necessary process would be of having a truly flexible system of personal constructs.

Therapeutic relationship

If the conclusion is that the way in which language is used reflects the conditional nature of our world, how can this be avoided in therapy? How can language adequately describe and convey feelings of abuse, confusion, rejection, self-loathing, loneliness, despair? How can therapists attempt to respond to the uniqueness of the client when they cannot convey their own? Is it possible within the therapeutic process for an opportunity to be created for therapist and client to develop a language between them that enables the client to explore who they really are and that closely reflects the client's true experience?

The relationship has been well acknowledged as the most important aspect of our therapeutic endeavours. 'Effectiveness of all types of therapy depends on the patient and the therapist forming a good relationship' (Department of Health 2004, ch 3.2, p. 36). Exploring the role of language in this is essential as it is through words that the self is described, and it is through words that the self defines others. It is through words that people most overtly make themselves available (or not) for relationship.

In trying to grasp what constitutes a therapeutic relationship Clarkson (1991) has given a comprehensive model, defining five modes of 'intentional relationship' in psychotherapy. Words are used differently in each of these modes as the focus deliberately moves between transference issues and developmental themes, the contract for therapy or the working alliance, the dialogic or real relationship and the transpersonal.

Although psychodynamic therapists may say that it is the transferential relationship that is most significant, humanistic modalities emphasize the dialogic and transpersonal as of prime importance. It is the qualities of empathy, acceptance, attunement, how therapists enquire about their clients and how they convey all of these things to the client as real person to real person, that build a relationship where a genuine dialogue can occur. From there can come shared moments of expansive awareness of the spiritual dimension of life. It is not the particular modality or theoretical understanding of the client's process, developmental or transferential revelations that the client remembers, but rather the less definable quality of the essence of what each individual therapist brought to the encounter.

The relatively new science of cybernetics has an interesting contribution to this subject. This developing field looks at how individual understandings of the world are communicated between people. Barnes (2001) relates cybernetics, as the science of communication, to psychotherapy, and considers what happens when two people talk to each other in the therapeutic process. He concludes that 'psychotherapy is a talking therapy which means that it heals through words'. In order to do this it has to use the words 'that are right for each individual patient ... they have to be the words that are right for healing a specific individual' (p. 539). Barnes refers to Buber (1967), who envisaged that a therapist who was able to respond so individually to each person would liberate the client from 'the unconscious imposition of therapists and of the concepts of their theories' (Barnes 2001: 540). Buber (1967) believed that it would then be possible to have therapists whom he described as 'musical' because they could respond with a different tune, different words for every individual patient. He added that 'the real master responds to uniqueness' (cited in Barnes 2001: 540).

Can the restrictions imposed by language really facilitate this uniqueness? Earlier chapters have demonstrated that language is not just a cognitive exercise; it is intertwined with the whole of human development. The relationship with language is a reflection of the emotional patterns of life.

Kurtz (2004) has likened the way a therapist has to suspend their own sense of self in order to enter fully into the experience of the client to that of an author of a creative novel who has to step clear of their world in order to build that of their fictional characters. This notion of stepping outside the personal world involves the therapist in being aware that the client is bringing a whole dictionary of their own. The therapist needs to be ready to accept the new definitions contained in this dictionary, the new meanings that a client might attach to a word. In trying to create a joint vocabulary of signs and symbols the therapeutic pair must co-construct a unique intersubjective field, stepping outside the familiar symbolic framework that they may have used all their lives to identify themselves and their place in the world, in order to understand and to value the other. The therapist needs to encourage the client to express these meanings and to give validity to them, creating space for new meaning. In working with clients one of the most effective interventions can be 'what does that word mean for you?' It is too easy for the therapist to assume that when a client says they are depressed or anxious their meaning is clear. The different modalities, and possibly Gestalt therapy in particular, see the pattern of language use as helpful for understanding the inner psyche. The way something is expressed can show how powerful or how weak the individual is feeling and can give power or take it away from the other.

The notions of cognitive imperialism and verbal bullying combined with the inherent inability of language to do justice to our inner affect make it a potent weapon against those most cherished and much applauded goals of all modalities of therapy: self-awareness, self-fulfilment, choice and change.

Bakhtin (1981) thought of therapy as a struggle to repress a dominant language. The dominant language in psychotherapy could be seen as that of the therapist, the powerful interpreter of the client's mystical processes. The client's voice, which relates to their own world, tries to suppress this powerful language in order to be heard. Yet therapists use words that have their own meaning imbued with the culture of the specific core modality. An important question is how Mollon's (2003) notion of cognitive imperialism is reinforced by the language that the therapist chooses to use. Just because the same words are used does not mean that they are used in the same way (Levenson 1991).

In the early 1980s Grove developed the therapeutic technique of 'clean language' (Tompkins and Lawley 1997). Having studied transcripts of therapy he recognized how the therapist changed the frame of reference of the client through a subtle rewording of what they had said. In trying not only to validate the client's experience but also to give it greater form he identified nine clean language questions. These questions request information about metaphors that a client uses and the symbols contained within them. They ask about the context of the metaphor in the here and now, in the past and in the future. Finally, by asking the client 'And that's . . . like what?' this offers them an opportunity to create another metaphor, which helps them to make a shift in perception. He found that the less he contaminated their description the more the clients experienced their own core patterns and made unexpected discoveries about themselves and their experiences. This led to the client having greater awareness of their own process, observing their own patterns and being able to make connections and insights.

Metaphor

The clean language technique is used in a form of therapy called symbolic modelling which also works with the metaphors and symbols that clients use. Lawley (Tompkins et al. 2005) describes this as recognizing the importance of working with a client's metaphorical language without contaminating it with that of the therapist.

The definition of metaphor that Lawley uses is taken from Lakoff and Johnson (1980): 'the essence of metaphor is understanding and experiencing one kind of thing in terms of another' (Tompkins et al. 2005: 33). He adds that a metaphor is seen as being made up of symbols, and much learning is available through exploring the metaphors and symbols that a client uses to express themselves: 'When a client uses a metaphor it contains the structural essence of their experience' (Tompkins et al. 2005). It can often be easier for a client to describe an intense emotional experience through metaphor. Referring back to the four senses of self in therapy identified by Forness-Bennett (1997), described in more detail in Chapter 3, the use of metaphor might be seen as a way of expressing the reflexive self as the client tries to contact their inner representational world.

By using clean questions to explore the metaphor with the client, 'the metaphor changes and evolves, the client's perception of the issues changes and the client learns to create new experience through the evolution of their metaphors and symbols' (Forness-Bennett 1997: 1).

Historically metaphor is the opposite of literal, changing the perspective of reality, transferring qualities between such opposed things as objects, emotions and activities. Following their research in 1980, Lakoff and Johnson (1999) suggested that underlying the huge amount of different metaphors found in everyday speech are a smaller number of conceptual metaphors. The conceptual metaphor is the foundational idea on which the metaphorical expression then builds. Lakoff believed that these conceptual metaphors derived from basic physical experience and understanding of the concrete world. This knowledge is then used to understand more abstract concepts such as emotions and time.

Eynon (2001) gives examples of six conceptual metaphors:

1. *time is money* ('don't waste my time', 'I spent too much time on that')
2. *activities are containers* ('I am in the middle of writing')
3. *knowing is seeing* ('do you see what I mean?', 'what is your view on that?')

4. *the part is the whole* ('the head of the company')
5. *attributes are objects* ('she got fatter and fatter')
6. *events are actions* ('the child came in to the world').

Some of these metaphors are so familiar that they are thought of as objective truth and are consequently accepted as real. There is however a falseness in this which reflects Lacan's assertion of the way in which language is allowed to trick its audience. Any magician understands the power of the conceptual metaphor, *'knowing is seeing'*, because of its capacity to deceive.

In the therapeutic context the word *transference* is commonly used to describe the transfer of affect from one situation to another. In this sense metaphor means the same as transference (Pedder 1979). Coming from Greek and Latin roots both metaphor and transference literally mean 'to carry across'. Holmes (2004: 215) describes transference as 'a special type of metaphor in which early childhood feelings are carried across into the relationship with the therapist'. Clearly there is a strong similarity between the idea of conceptual metaphors and the unconscious belief systems that are worked with in therapy. A metaphor used by a client offers much information about how that person views the world.

In the dream described in Chapter 3 the rat could be understood as the conceptual metaphor, *'anger is a dangerous animal'* (Eynon 2001). The dreamer was angry at being challenged over her lack of interaction. The challenge threatened her by inviting her into a new, untried and untested way of being, challenging an unconscious belief that she had grown up with and making an unthought known into a known thought.

Spirituality

> It can be argued that psychotherapy is ultimately a spiritual project.
>
> (King-Spooner 2001: 28).

Buber's 'I–Thou' has come to be regarded as the ultimate indication of a therapeutic relationship – a transpersonal/spiritual experience embedded in the interpersonal. In order to achieve this person-to-person attitude the psychotherapist must 'stand again and again not merely at his own pole in the bipolar reaction but also with the strength of present realisation at the other pole', and it can only be done by 'one who grasps the buried latent unity of the suffering soul' (Buber 1958: 90). The theme of connectedness in this description of the I–Thou experience is also apparent in chaos theory, which emphasizes the interconnectedness of all life. Yet language divides things up, shaping them into manageable pieces. It is therefore ultimately in conflict with the essence of a more spiritual view of the world which sees variation and connection between everything (Clarkson 2001).

Clarke (2001) wrote of psychosis and spirituality as on the same continuum, yet language conceptualizes them differently. Psychosis is a diagnostic term and as such emphasizes the danger of a psychotic state of mind. The word comes with concepts about how psychosis should be treated as an illness and dealt with to keep society safe. Spirituality on the other hand is something to be aspired to. It is positive and welcomed as a better way of being. One is a medical word, the other is connected with society's traditions of faith and religion. They are both states of mind where reason and logic give way to mystery and the unknown. But in western culture they are treated differently. The words used to describe these two states of mind divide them. This limiting or 'bitting' (Clarke 2001) aspect to language is summed up by Heath (2002) in this way: 'Words are not in direct correspondence to reality either external or experiential. There is always a gap between words and that to which they are applied' (p. 13). Speech can enliven or it can deaden (Wright 2006). What makes it do one or the other is the language used. Do the words live in order to connect/reconnect with people at a spiritual level?

Conclusion

Words are given power by the way in which they are used. Original meanings can be distorted and diluted through words.

The word 'care' comes from the same root as 'courage', that is, from the heart. So what does it mean to care about clients? 'Intimacy' is from the same root as 'intimate', to hint at. So does wanting closeness also connect with a desire for mystery, to have some flavour of the mystery of the other? Perhaps the process of therapy is this longing to enter into the mystery of the other (Orlando-Fantini 2005).

Does the way that language is used in therapy reflect this longing? Language is limited and carries with it an accumulation of all the prejudices and assumptions and imperfections that permeate the whole history of the human race. It is full of cultural chauvinism and cognitive imperialism. It is heavy with the imposition of the expectations of others. It is changeable and restrictive, creating an illusion of reality that acts as a block against experiencing the reality that is constantly sought. It creates social and cultural barriers and is, fatally, what society is built upon. The basic human condition described by Lacan of not knowing the truth is institutionalized by language. It is 'complicit in conveying and engendering and nurturing and promulgating and celebrating the pathological modes of human being' (Pyle 1977).

In the same way that language has been described as a double-edged sword for the child, so it can be seen as having the same awkward potential for both helping and hindering the process in the therapy room. Green (1979/2004: 229) said that language is 'situated between the cry and silence'. Perhaps talking and anxiety are closely connected. Beginning to say something about what is thought, felt, experienced or believed can be like jumping into an abyss. Often there is not time to completely formulate all of what needs to be said. The client is not like the public speaker or lecturer with their notes. Rather, a risk is taken, based on assumptions about possible reactions. Words come with ready-made definitions attached to them. Silence comes without any such encumbrance. It is easier to be much more tentative and enquiring in discovering the meaning in silence. Silence can be thought of as a protection of our words from misinterpretation and attack (Sabbadini 2004: 232). That silence can be safer is a belief that is held by many shy, timid, and quiet people. Sabbadini goes further and describes silence as part of language which can express many emotions. However, it is also true that the process of trying to describe feelings verbally can assist a sense of identity, as thoughts and feelings are revealed to the self and to the other (Russell 1989). Language creates a space in which to share publicly something that has been observed or felt or believed to be true, or to have been experienced in some way. All this is recognized by the different therapeutic modalities, which agree that the language of a client reflects their basic stance towards the world.

A number of questions nonetheless remain. How possible is it ultimately to achieve real connection through words? Does language actually prevent real connection? Or are the words of novelist Thomas Hardy (1874/1974) ultimately true: 'He would as soon have thought of carrying an odour in a net as of attempting to convey the intangibilities of his feeling in the coarse meshes of language' (p. 58)?

CHAPTER 6

Agendered language: does language have a gender – and an agenda – of its own?

Nicola Barden

The question of whether language constitutes or reflects identity is nowhere more clear than at the birth of a baby. Once breathing and health are established, the genitals come under the gaze of the midwife/parent; the cry of 'it's a girl' or 'it's a boy' follows. It is a quick glance for such a profound label. In the move from the seeing to the naming, the embodiment to the linguistic, a world of difference is brought to play. It is evidenced very concretely – choice of name, colour of clothing, the manner in which the baby is held and spoken about (and to). It is held in the mind of family and friends as they begin to form hopes for the future. Systems will swing into action to ensure clarity of sex identification. Expectations will begin.

Even when a parent is determined not to act on pre-ascribed gender roles the very fact that they must consciously avoid them means that they are present. Present, that is, to all but the infant, who for the first year to 18 months has little or no awareness of gender identity but by 3 years finds that it is fixed in the manner of feeling a fundamental belonging to one or the other group, male or female (Vas Dias 2001). Gender awareness initially develops on an unconscious level, or most certainly a non-verbal one, as it coheres at the same time as vocabulary and language skills are allowing the toddler to make sense of their world. Naturally, much sense has been made already, but not a communicated, shared sense, where ownership and mastery of their experience can come through the naming of it. This is not a simple growing into something. The gender identity understood by the young child at this point is already far removed from the naming of genitals. It has already become a part of where they feel they belong in the naming of the world, and as they too continue with the naming they both inhabit and create it. Indeed, they have no opportunity to do otherwise, for where is there to sit outside of gender, yet still to be recognized, still exist in the linguistic community of humankind? In Lacanian terms, one may be born male or female through biology, but one becomes a man or a woman through speaking (Soler 2000).

Focusing on gender, this chapter will look closely at how language creates and reflects existence, and underline the need for awareness of how words are used in the consulting room.

Body language

It might be thought that the body at least is obvious, that if there are issues of language and naming that there is in the flesh a real object underlying those questions, an object that in its very reality can be picked up, cuddled, played with and related to, and that constitutes enough reality to make all the questions about gender seem a little, well, irrelevant. The problem with this approach lies in the concept of reciprocity implied in the descriptions of cuddling, playing and relating. To reciprocate, the body must be subject as well as object. The 'out-there' existence cannot occur separately from the relational existence, but rather is brought into existence by it – Winnicott's (1960a/1990) point that there is no such thing as a baby, only a mother-and-baby: '*the inherited potential of an infant cannot become an infant unless linked to maternal care*' (p. 43). The parent *perceives* the baby. She or he cannot perceive the baby directly, but only through their own capacity to receive and understand. The baby cannot even perceive itself directly, but must come into psychic being through a mirroring relationship to others: 'Until the grasp of language, the infant's meaning resides in the mind and body of the mother' (Rutherford 1992: 109). Therefore the infant can only be the infant that is in the mind of its carers when it is being thought of by them, because that is the self it sees mirrored back; and the parents cannot think of the infant from a place outside of their own thoughts. Into their perception of the baby will come that which is already in their minds in preparation for thinking about it; in their perception of the baby's gender will come all that which is already in their thinking about gender. The baby's gender does not belong to the baby; it belongs immediately to the gendered world, mediated by language. As it becomes a gendered subject it feeds back into language, contributes to it, and becomes both constituent and constitutor of gender.

In this way the words 'boy' and 'girl' begin to define a state rather than describe it. What is actually constructed through language is received as if part of a natural order. What falls outside of the labels is experienced as unnatural, and this is indicated by the use of 'outsider' words (tomboy, sissy) or even no words at all: if there is no word for something it cannot exist or be recognized. 'Outsider' words put the object beyond the realm of the normal simply through limiting the way in which it can be talked about. There is no admiring way in mainstream language to describe an effeminate boy.

A good demonstration of this role of language in gender definition can be found in the response of society to bodies that do not fit straightforwardly into the boy/girl category at infancy. It can be argued that these existences are a small minority – some estimate 1 in 30,000 (Bing and Bergvall 1998); that language is based on commonality and consensus; that no harm or meaning is intended in concentrating on the majority. Yet there is arguably a significant meaning in the inability of language to allow for a discourse associated with what, for the want of a better term, is described as 'intersex'. The word is interesting as it presupposes two sexes that an individual may fall between, being in that case neither one thing nor the other. A parallel awkwardness is found in words describing children with racially mixed parentage. 'Mixed race' implies the existence of a pure race at either end and does not reflect the diversity of racial mix that is in everyone. It does not question the assumption of there being definable races. Yet if an individual is to be named it must be within the limiting category of racial description that language allows. American definitions of 'black' dating from the days of slavery counted the existence of one black ancestor going back three generations, which shows clearly how naming can be deeply political while being portrayed as natural.

The refusal to name is a useful indicator of exclusion: 'Although the birth of intersexed individuals is not rare, it is unmentionable, even in tabloids that regularly report such outrageous topics as copulation with extraterrestrials and the reappearance of Elvis' (Bing and Bergvall 1998: 501). The point is not whether something is in the minority or the majority, but whether language allows it a place in the realm of that which exists. If language reflected only the condition of the object, sexes would be neither binary nor opposite. Using the word 'opposite' itself maintains the binary by placing all variation within one spectrum at the same time as affirming the distance between the two ends. At no point has intersex been granted a place of its own, not subject to the dominant discourse of sex, but simply there in its own right. The very word is a diagnostic category. Nor has it been allowed to influence the language that exists. Having man/woman, masculine/feminine on a spectrum is an ostensibly liberal but actually conservative manoeuvre which maintains the status quo while appearing to broaden it. It seems preferable to fit difference into existing concepts of normal rather than to alter the concepts. The control of language is in this sense the control of reality – though not of ideas, which work their way into subversive discourses and alternative vocabularies.

The response to intersex infants continues to be a medical one of first 'assigning' the sex and then altering the body to fit. The procedures are generally quite unnecessary in health terms; their purpose is to provide a liveable, sexed body for the individual. With all its difficulties it is still believed to be better for someone to have a surgically altered life as a clearly identifiable man or woman than to live in an ambiguous body. This illustrates the power of language as a container and shaper of social experience. Sourcing gender definitions in biology is seen as common sense, and the natural world is frequently quoted in evidence of this. But even zoology has been as much a participant in culture-bound gender expectations as any other branch of science. Because animal 'homosexuality', as Bagemihl (1999) describes it – meaning variously having sex, setting up home, rearing young together – runs directly counter to the assumption that heterosexuality is the natural result of having two sexes, the only way to keep up the 'naturalness', rather than consider the construction, of sex is to emphasize the unnaturalness of the ill-fitting behaviour. Studies on both animal and human homosexuality look for abnormality, whether physical or psychological, an abnormality that is arguably diversity by another name. Anatomical studies of human homosexual bodies in the nineteenth and twentieth centuries searched for enlarged clitorises in women, unusual fat deposits in men, to capture definitive distinctions between gay and straight bodies. This itself mirrored the shameful 'scientific' examination of particularly black African bodies by western doctors keen to define racial difference (Somerville 2000; Barden 2001).

What begins to emerge is a picture of sex that represents much more than the sexed infant before it. Language carries a wealth of associated and often unconscious meanings: 'Gendered statuses are such powerful political, legal and ideological constraints on an individual's sexuality and emotional relationships that alternative statuses are almost unthinkable' (Lorber 1994: 79). Politics, law and ideology are contained in the word, which carries multiple meanings.

With men and women as unassailable categories, masculine and feminine likewise become fixed, the inalienable characteristics of one or the other sex. Later efforts made some headway in seeing masculine and feminine as at least in part socially influenced in their content, but their early use as definitive terms is demonstrated in a 1960s study by Strauss, who observed the manner in which boys and girls threw balls. The girls threw without force, speed or aim; the boys threw with acceleration and direction. As they were only 5 year olds, Strauss felt he could not put this down to any particular influence, so he said it must be down to the 'feminine attitude' in relation to the world and space. Young (2005), recounting this tale, puts it down to what little girls and boys have already taken in about their being in the world: 'Women in sexist society are physically handicapped'; they are 'inhibited, confined, positioned, objectified' (p. 42). Women, she suggests, do not move as if the world belongs to them, because it does not. That is why the boys could throw the ball as if they owned the space around them. Although Young accounts for the difference in social terms, Strauss was able to put it in essentialist terms – somehow this was just about being a girl. Once the word 'man', or 'masculine', is accepted with all its political and ideological meanings, it becomes a natural thing that a boy should throw like a man, who owns the world, and a girl should throw like a woman, who does not.

Words are contradictory in this sense. At one extreme, a girl means a body with a clitoris less than one inch long and viable reproductive organs, and all other characteristics are secondary to this. At the other extreme, a girl means a person who demonstrates a host of thoughts, feelings and behaviours associated with femininity. The word 'girl' becomes the unifying factor for a range of meanings which otherwise might fracture apart. The word becomes bigger than the sum of its parts as 'girl' then *creates* the entity that it was originally just attempting to *describe*. Being a girl becomes an explanation of difference; the word takes on authority in its own right.

Negotiation of this conundrum depends on an awareness of living in a constructed world, an approach much more possible in the current post-modern era with its multiple realities than in the philosophies that underlay the modernist approach. Yet therapy, psychoanalysis in particular, developed in the modernist era and this influences its search for a single satisfactory Oedipal outcome, although it could be said that Freud was less concerned about this than many of his immediate followers.

Sex, sexuality and gender present real difficulties in being adequately captured by language. Because the name of something affects the manner in which it can be thought about, naming is more than 'mere' semantics. When the underlying structures are flawed, moving the words around does not provide a solution. Strenuous efforts have been made to tie gender down, whether in terms of male/female, masculine/feminine, or gay/straight. Yet individual lives appear not to conform to this ideal. In the body there is intersex. In personality, no one is all masculine or all feminine, even were it possible to reach agreement on what that means. In orientation, sexuality can change substantially over a single lifetime for many people.

Even in this chapter the terms 'sex', 'gender' and 'sexual identity' have been used inconsistently, or at least, to mean more than one thing. This appears unclear and frustrating. It is however reflective of the linguistic confusion between sex, gender and sexuality. Scientific studies describe animal homosexual behaviour with unacknowledged anthropomorphism: rams deem it an 'insult' to be mounted; egrets 'suffer' same-sex activity; grouse are 'victims'; orang-utans are 'forced'; ducks are 'seduced'; butterflies lower their 'moral standards' (Bagemihl 1999: 90–1). These animals apparently have a gender identity to protect, which is threatened by sexual identity. This can only be a projection of the human position. The search for bodily difference, if it could be found, offers the solution that these are not 'real' male sheep or male orang-utans, but a sort of male–female intermediate. This is no further on than the work of the German sexual liberationist, Ulrichs, in the late nineteenth century (Bristow 1997) who believed that same-sex attraction was a case of a female mind inhabiting a man's body, a sort of third sex. There is still no construct for 'real man' that includes the concept 'homosexual', or 'real woman' that includes 'lesbian'. When an individual brings themselves into an encounter as a lesbian or gay man they will inevitably undergo a little desexing. Television shows are now made of the 'can you guess?' variety, that is, can a gay man pass sufficiently for straight to fool a heterosexual woman? The assumption is that 'gay' would contradict 'man', so an act is required. Not only are bodies gendered, but so are desires (Bristow 1997). Freud's (1932/1990) recognition of this issue was clear if at times contradictory:

> We are accustomed to employ 'masculine' and 'feminine' as mental qualities as well [as physical], and have in the same way transferred the notion of bisexuality to mental life. Thus we speak of a person, whether male or female, as behaving in a masculine way in one connection and in a feminine way in another. But you will soon perceive that this is only giving way to anatomy or to

convention . . . I advise you against it. It seems to me to serve no useful purpose and to add nothing to our knowledge.

(pp. 344–5)

Desire

Not only are bodies gendered but so are desires (Bristow 1997). Fitting sexual desire into the same linguistic order as sexual identity is facilitated by the concept of heterosexual complementarity (Butler 1990, 1993). The differences between men and women are balanced by each being able to possess traits of the other gender, to make a whole. The question remains why, if a woman performs a 'masculine' act, is it masculine? What does it take for something to become 'feminine' if it is not the performing of it by a woman?

Modern anthropologists study biology as the raw material for gender systems and recognize that the content of what is definitive varies, although the existence of a system for definition is ubiquitous. Sexuality is something that stands for more than itself. 'Because sexuality in Western societies is so mystified, the wars over it are often fought at oblique angles, aimed at phony targets, conducted with misplaced passions, and are highly, intensely symbolic. Sexual activities often function as signifiers for personal and social apprehensions to which they have no intrinsic connection' (Rubin 1993: 25). Sexuality is named by culture for cultural ends. Like most naming it has the purpose of capturing, freezing, holding still. This push towards linguistic immobility does not well suit experiences that are fluid and variable, but it does manage the fear of chaos, fragmentation and death that underpins the defensive anxieties that such fluidity arouses. If this process of management is more important than the meaning of the words, then the war is indeed fought at an angle. Sex, gender and desire are set up as if causally related (Butler 1990). The feminine heterosexual female desires the masculine heterosexual male. Variance from one part of the equation demands balance from another. Butler's argument is that this is so tightly woven that it looks natural. Of course lesbians are going to be labelled as 'butch' or 'femme' because it keeps the gender paradigm in place; of course gay men will be labelled 'effeminate' and thus part woman, part man. Language will tie itself in knots in the service of stability. As Spender (1998) writes, language is a symbolic system and symbols are approximations. If used as reality they 'beguile us into accepting some of the most bizarre rules for making sense of the world. It is our capacity to symbolize and the use (or misuse) we make of the symbols we construct that constitutes the area of language, thought and reality' (p. 93).

Feinberg (1996) quotes a conversation with a reporter:

> 'You were born female, right?' The reporter asked me for the third time. I nodded patiently. 'So do you identify as female now, or male?' She rolled her eyes as I repeated my answer. 'I am trans-gendered. I was born female, but my masculine gender expression is seen as male. It's not my sex that defines me, and it's not my gender expression. Do you understand? It's the social contradiction between the two that defines me.' The reporter's eyes glazed over as I spoke. When I finished she said, 'So you're a *third* sex?' Clearly, I realized, we had very little language with which to understand each other.
>
> (p. 101)

The frustration is felt on both sides. The fault is neither Feinberg's nor the reporter's, but the restrictions placed by having to use the available language to explain a position that is not recognized by language. The explanation becomes leaden and, to the reporter, bizarre. Feinberg has no category of recognition therefore exists only outside of the society. A straightforward example is public lavatories. The only choice is male or female – there is no other door to walk through, yet for Feinberg neither door can be walked through. This circles back to Butler's point that gender, defined by culture, does not necessarily follow from sex. If language only develops within the acceptance of a binary system for sex and gender it will inevitably be limited in its rendition of experience: 'When the constructed status of gender is theorized as radically independent of sex, gender itself becomes a free-floating artifice, with the consequence that *man* and *masculine* might just as easily signify a female body as a male one, and *woman* and *feminine* a male body as easily as a female one' (Butler 1990: 6).

The words available simply do not describe experience, and the general conservatism of psychotherapy is slow to recognize new terminology when it does arise. Wilchins (2004: 39) lists words that describe some of the emerging gender identities: boy chick, no-ho tranny boys, faggot-identified dyke, andros, trykes, bio-femmes. This vocabulary is out there, lively and challenging, part of a fast-developing culture on the edge of lived gender identities. It has little articulation with traditional therapeutic language. Would a no-ho tranny boy (transsexual male not taking hormones) be able to talk to a therapist and be understood without the words being measured as deviations from the norm at one end, or listened to with goodwill but no search-ing exploration of meaning at the other? Definition is to be found as much at the edges as in the centre (Halberstam 1998). Words that sit at the edges of experience help to define the limits of existing vocabu-lary and existing concepts. When the concepts no longer represent experience it is likely to be more useful to broaden the concept than limit the experience.

This returns the debate to the limits of masculine and feminine discourse, and its enactment in the body, in materiality. It is clear that language does more than describe experience: it shapes it by maintaining the categories through which experience can be com-municated. Because sex, gender and sexuality have become contin-gent on one another, existing as a sexed, gendered and sexual subject is limited to the field within which these three things can be held in a relatively undisturbed relation to each other. That which is too disturbing finds itself outside of the place of recognition and order, into a place of non-existence in terms of being a subject. This can be uncovered by a consideration of these 'abject' zones (Butler 1990) such as intersex, transgender, transvestism. The border between words and wordlessness indicates the boundary of the habitable. This bound-ary may purport to draw the picture of sex and gender but it is likely to show rather the patterns of power and dominance in which sex and gender are situated. 'Agendered' language is part of the pattern weave.

Gender in language

Views on the different ways in which women and men use lan-guage tend to agree on the existence of difference but not on what it consists of.

Kaplan (1998) posits that differences between male and female speech become clear at puberty. Female language remains more child-like, seen but not heard, not fully grown up as girls are not allowed to grow up. Lakoff (1975) put it that all children are taught the language of women, and boys then unlearn it. In poorer countries education is still reserved for males. In wealthy countries women were held back from education as they were unlikely to need it, and it could give them ideas beyond their station. The link between lan-guage, education and liberty becomes clear when remembering that it was a crime to teach a slave to write (Cameron 1998). Boys, however, according to Kaplan (1998), were prepared to enter the adult domain and so were given freedom from childish constraints in adult talk, entering the man's world of obscenities and rough jokes. Although this is ameliorated by social moves towards equality, in much analytic theory women still inhabit a more difficult relationship to adulthood. They come from a position of what they do not have, that is the penis/phallus, and so can never be in the same zone as men, and to deny this is in itself seen as an impediment to resolving it. So the girl is caught in a revolving door which at each turn seems to eject her just before she assumes power. The boy is ejected firmly onto the board-room floor, whether he likes it or not. If language belongs to men, women have to put themselves in a position of subjugation if they want to speak at all. Take for example a phone call to a bank, where the woman is asked if she is Mrs, Miss or Ms. There is no way to answer this without being implicated in gendered power structures; even refusing to answer recognizes the question, and thus the relative positions of speaker and listener, leaving the woman ultimately without title.

Others (Cixous, Kristeva, Irigaray) accept the difference but reject the implication of inferiority, asserting the uniqueness of female language. Within a Lacanian framework the girl would still be in the realm of the mother and so in a pre-Oedipal place. This would be reflected in a language that was less about mastery and more about questioning and understanding (Mills 1998). This can seem somewhat passive, but describes what is rather than what might be. Social change can create and be brought about by linguistic change: 'If women are to accede to a different sort of social organisation, they need a religion, a language, and either a currency of their own or a non-market economy. These three conditions go hand in hand' (Irigaray, cited in Whitford 1991: 169).

This idea that language can create change as well as reflect it goes back to the Sapir–Whorf controversy discussed in Chapter 1. What Sapir and Whorf were perhaps less able to articulate was the dimension of power relations in the construction of language, and the subsequent creation of a double-bind effect for men and women: 'If you leave out power, you do not understand any talk' (Troemel-Ploetz 1998). Language structure reflects social practices, but is used as if it has a moral authority of its own. Those who are motivated to speak out against the prevailing use of language will be those it serves less well, and feminist readings of language argue that in gender terms this means women. Those with most power to alter the dominant discourse, in these terms men, are likely to have a more protectionist stance towards the status quo, and to undermine or resist change. It is not quite as simple as that, of course. The days when it can be said that a woman means yes when she says no have passed (although a Canadian Supreme Court Judge did say as recently as 1991 that it might mean 'maybe', or 'wait a while' (Ehrlich and King 1998: 164)), and this is as a result of successful activism by women that has changed how people think, to a degree, and this has then influenced what is spoken. At the same time, attempts to alter the use of 'he' as a generic term to encompass men and women is still seen as strident and ridiculous, an unnecessary struggle against established practice which is without gender significance. 'He/she' or 'they' have been denounced as inelegant alternatives, attempts to fundamentally change language – which in a sense they are. However, language had already been changed, by the Act of Parliament of 1850 which legally replaced 'he or she' with 'he', ostensibly to shorten the number of words used overall in long acts of legislation (Bodine 1998). Efforts to bring racist language to attention have been similarly pushed aside – the constant association between whiteness, brightness and goodness, while dark and black represents evil, for example, have been dismissed as excessively sensitive nonsense. Although there has been some impact on public speech and language it has not altered the cultural consciousness which now portrays itself as rather beleaguered and under assault through the phrase 'political correctness'. Thus the most powerful discourse prevails and undermines change: 'If the group in which the change originated was not the highest-status group in the speech community, members of the highest status group eventually stigmatized the changes through their social control of various institutions of the communication network' (Labov 1972: 179). Change requires a move in power relations; language is power, and does not move easily.

In safe situations men and women, girls and boys, reveal aspects of their gender identity that are not normally spoken of. Research interviews with adolescent boys in London (Frosh et al. 2002) demonstrated that when given space with a sensitive male interviewer they were not at all the inarticulate, grunting stereotype of adolescence, but eloquent and thoughtful individuals. Many expressed a longing for a father figure that had not been matched by the reality, and were saddened by the loss of this potential. They felt that the ideal of masculinity was constraining yet it was impossible to do anything other than conform to it. This was crystal clear in terms of sexuality – it would have been impossible to be openly gay and to survive. The homophobia was partly about a fear of femininity, as being not-a-girl was of major importance in being seen to be masculine; there was no room for anything that could be heard as feminine. Masculinity was also linked to culture and ethnicity in complex ways. African Caribbean boys for example had high masculine status (hard, sporty, cool, not interested in schoolwork) but were denigrated in racial terms.

These interviews demonstrated the performative nature of gender. The boys described not what it *was*, as an external force, but more how they *did* it, how gender was brought into being by their performance of what was expected of them. Subverting gender – which they actually did in the interviews, in which they were generally not hard or unemotional or unworried about their lives – was only possible outside the interviews at cost of a masculine identity. They could act masculine as required, but it was not their only performance nor necessarily their favourite one.

Gender in therapeutic discourse

The boys demonstrated that gender is enacted, brought into being by a continued system of small enactments that together contribute an edifice so monumental and sure of itself that it has taken on the mantle of truth and reality. Language is a daily participant in this construction. Feminism has been a harsh critic of this structure, and post-modernism an able opponent. But post-modernism too shall fade. The solution is not to find 'the' post-modernist position on therapeutic gender discourse, but to be alive to the changing nuances and be receptive to an ever-changing place within them, at least for the foreseeable future, and to recognize therapeutic language as gendered.

There are power constructs in therapeutic relationships. Indeed, it would be remarkable if there were not. Some therapies work consciously to address and reduce the power imbalance, emphasizing the work as a cooperative venture with the client as the expert; others use the dynamic as grist to the transferential mill and see it as a valuable part of the process. All acknowledge that there is a power issue to be negotiated in the consulting room, with a potential for misuse, not least through professionalizing conversation so that the words themselves become a demonstration of power rather than a means of communication, as discussed in Chapter 5. In addition to this inbuilt dynamic are the actual persons of the therapist and the client, who have to negotiate their individual power relationship across similarities and differences including ethnicity, social class, gender, sexuality, and so on. The most unhelpful thing perhaps is if either party nurture the belief that these differences are left behind at the consulting room door, or that they are 'only' about the people in the room. The room is part of the world – this is Butler's (1990) insistent point, that there is no stepping aside, no sanctuary, no other place to go. Evidence across theoretical orientations (Wampold 2001) concludes that the relationship between client and counsellor is integral to therapeutic efficacy. It is through the relationship that they will hear each other's words, whether this is cast as the counsellor's congruence, or their honest attention to their counter-transference, and language cannot be heard or spoken without reference to the hearer and speaker. In gender terms, both parties exist within the framework of their personal and cultural gender norms, and dialogue must take place with reference to these positions.

Frosh (1994: 116) discusses a moment in working with a couple where the man talked for a quarter of an hour about his own story and future plans without referring to his wife, who then unexpectedly and inarticulately began weeping, only able to utter the word 'nobody . . .' (later concluded as 'nobody would be interested') and then at the end, '. . . sorry'. Frosh notes the gender relevance of the interaction, that there are two men in the room, now silent as she weeps, the husband having excluded her from his history and his future, the therapist unable to form a response. He considers the possibility that the woman's most powerful tool may be her silence; that in the presence of the men language may not serve her, as her role is to listen, to be the listening female. The husband takes up his place within language; the wife takes up her place outside of it. The therapist is aware, but has to react from within the construct, or be silent.

In this encounter Frosh demonstrates that it is not only the *content* of language that will demonstrate gender but also its *process*. Many studies have evidenced difference in men's and women's speech patterns. Universals are hard to prove, but Holmes (1998) suggests function, solidarity and power as three possible contenders. In brief, men are likely to concentrate on content, information, things, activities; women on feelings and relationships. Women's conversation tends to offer more feedback and invite response more frequently. Men's conversation tends to be about holding the floor and is more interrupting. Tannen (1992) generalizes further and suggests that men's talk is focused on maintaining autonomy and status, while women concentrate on promoting connection and intimacy, and it is the different but unacknowledged aims of each partner that makes cross-gender conversations so confusing and sometimes frustrating. There can be a sort of hopelessness in this, that women will be weeping victims and men the thoughtless tyrants, but that sort of characterization is not helpful in the therapy room. What is helpful is for the therapist to be able to see their position inside the dominant gender discourse and to engage with it, not to think themselves beyond or outside of it. Frosh (1994) in his reflections considered his position specifically as a male therapist in that encounter, and could then be open to the dynamic that may have been created for both the husband and the wife. The therapeutic response comes not from neutrality but from within.

The therapeutic discourse is necessarily exploratory, tentative, and so suits an uncertain position in relation to gender. Gender certainty is arguably the most dubious standpoint for clinician or client. The comparative rigidity of the binary structures – male/female, masculine/feminine, gay/straight – do no justice to the fluidity of sex or gender or sexuality that is typical of the human experience. Yet language has embedded them, is embedded in them, so that it has been difficult to speak from any other position. Experience has been constrained when it is vocabulary that should have been broadened.

The idea of a spectrum gives limited flexibility, and other models have been proposed – intersecting circles of race, class, sexuality (West and Fenstermaker 1995), or threads in a tapestry (Nicholson 1994). These propose a messier picture of gender and are more injected with the sense of life that comes from instability.

Therapists must engage with themselves as gendered subjects in order to respond to their client as gendered beings. Empathy comes from the ability to see self in other as well as self distinct from other, and to hold both positions at once. Considering empathy across racial or ethnic differences between client and counsellor, Adams (1996: 191) suggests that 'empathy does not entail a denial of difference – by an appeal, for example, to a common "human nature" ', but requires looking to the self for a 'transpositional imitation', something from within that can link to the other's experience. When the divisions of gender insist that we distinguish one from the other in order to be one or the other it is difficult to own that which could provide the transpositional imitation. A man may be in touch with his feminine side, but by putting it this way places it outside of himself, preserving the conceptual ideal of the real masculine as a 'thing' rather than a 'doing', and not acknowledging its construction. The phrases to impugn a man's masculinity relate to crossed gender and sexuality roles – 'pussy whipped', 'faggoty', 'big girl's blouse'. For women likewise – 'ball breaker', 'butch', 'bulldyke'. The therapist needs to be prepared to inhabit these zones of exclusion in order to cross into the land of the other gender, to communicate an understanding of the gendered being of the other that will be experienced as authentic. This means struggling with language, finding words that describe experience rather than fitting experience into the words. This chapter has focused on gender, but there are parallels with all excluded groups. There are no words for example that describe disabilities without positioning them against a superior concept of ability. This is why some groups are so passionate about language – without it they appear not to exist, and with it their existence is defined in ways that are not recognizable. It is not that finding the right word will make all the difference, but the process of bringing the word into language will itself alter consciousness.

Conclusion

Language gathers life into words and channels it through rules in order to make communication possible. The price of communication is approximation; the other cannot be known directly. But there is a tendency to forget this. Words should not be confused with life; they are there to serve and not to rule. Gender as it is lived is not yet well articulated. Yet the words are doing their job – they describe the life that it is allowable to live. Therapists need to be able to understand the difference.

Epilogue – or after the word

Two aspects of communication stand out for me when I reflect on the process of writing. The first is how I communicate – my relationship with words and symbols and how this affects me in all aspects of my life as well as in being a therapist. The second is the differences in communication between different therapeutic modalities. I will start with the latter.

I have been trained as an integrative psychotherapist, using a model based on a combination of humanistic self-psychology and the psychoanalytic, with a strong relational focus. During my training I learned much about my lack of confidence with words, with speaking, and much about my openness in relationship and acceptance of change and difference. My choice of an integrative training reflected my stance in the world of wanting to be open to many different experiences.

My co-author is a psychoanalytic therapist. Perhaps rather harshly, a very experienced therapist once described to me the difference between humanistic and psychoanalytic therapists as their respective attitudes towards relationship. The humanistic therapist moves forward towards relationship while the psychoanalyst moves away from it. If this were true the two modalities at their extremes would be opposing forces. If it were true, then how can two people coming from these different modalities work closely enough together to write a book? Perhaps it is because even if this therapist spoke from experience, and my experience would support what he said, I do not view one as right and the other as wrong. I would not say that it is better to be one or the other, although clearly my personal preference is for the humanistic position. I believe that somewhere in the middle lies the correct relational stance and that we can only get to the middle by learning from each other. That involves not being defensive or threatened by a different point of view.

For example, throughout my writing I struggled with putting everything in the third person. Constantly Nicola has commented on my writing too much in the first person. She spoke, of course, at such times from an academic perspective, about the style of the series, and not as a psychoanalytic psychotherapist. My style comes from my natural instinct to take responsibility for my role in saying or doing anything. This can often mean that I am too subjective and too sensitive and at worst I expect criticism. If this is tempered with a more impersonal, objective approach, then it can mean that there is actually more space for both myself and for the other, as the humanist in me moves to a position where I can stand back from relationship in order to maintain the validity of my own individuality rather than to prove it. The psychoanalyst in turn can also embrace the opposite approach, so that he or she is more ready for relationship without feeling that their individuality is threatened. How we use words in therapy reflects all this, as we have shown in our exploration of the role of words in the different modalities. As I trained to become a therapist I also learned how much of myself I closed off to life because of my timidity with words. During the process of writing I have become much more aware of the power of words, with their ability to impact upon our lives and our experience of the world. Not being confident enough to speak up often means getting passed over. Not being able to shout loud and clearly enough when you need to can mean having to stay on the periphery of life.

As a result of this aspect of my personality one of my constant struggles throughout has been with the word count. I struggle with saying more than is absolutely necessary since my preference is for keeping my time on the soap box to a minimum. As a result I can often feel I have stopped short of explaining myself fully. As a new writer, and as a humanistic therapist, this is a personal challenge, to literally take up more space.

In the therapeutic relationship, even when I think I am doing my utmost not to impact the client's process, I am in fact contaminating it just by opening my mouth. I know that this is unavoidable, but what I had not appreciated before was the subtlety of it and how important it is to take that into account in the therapeutic process. It is another influential factor that will have an effect on the relationship between me and the person with whom I am working. I knew before embarking on this book how important it is to try to understand every aspect of the therapeutic relationship, but I have been struck by how easy it is not to question the essence of our communication, such as the words that we use.

Sometimes the very words used to explain concepts and experiences themselves need explaining by more words. Words, words, words. But I have learned to question more whether we are clear about what those words mean, and whether when we use words we all mean the same thing. How can we ever know for certain that we understand each other? In everyday life this matters but in the therapeutic relationship, where the aim is to understand the experience of the other and to help the other to feel understood, it is crucial. We can deceive ourselves into thinking our clients leave with a better understanding of themselves because our interventions have been based on what they say. We make interventions based on what we think or feel the client means, but actually are we not just masters at guess work? Whether it is solely through the words, or some other form of expression such as music, art or drama, we use different clues to help us with our guesses. Perhaps analysis of our most common form of communication is an ever decreasing circle into which we are reluctant to step.

And having stepped into it I have become more aware of how we use labels. I have really come to understand the power of labelling and its capacity to give an identity to a person or a group. On the one hand this can give power to people by giving them a recognized place in culture. On the other it can be disempowering by imposing a false, minimizing identity.

This journey of mine into words and symbols has provided me with many insights. It has also inevitably raised more questions. The opportunities that come from our different ways of communicating, both on an obvious and a more subtle level, have to be set against the limitations of trying to communicate the incommunicable. In addition to the value of my own journey through these matters, I conclude with my hope that the reader too has gained from what we have written, and is generous enough to understand when words have failed us.

Tina Williams

As we conclude our book, I naturally reflect upon the text itself. It is the space to consider the mediated nature of experience that has been most significant for me. I had always thought rather naïvely that children learned language through imitating their parents. This seems not to be the case. Language is created, not imitated. It is something that people do with the same innate necessity as breathing. It is the medium through which we make ourselves known. Some things are easier to put into words than others; some communication needs to be based on images or sounds in order to make sense. All communication, however, is based on the principle of language, of one thing standing in for another. This is the way in which we communicate our being. Because we can consciously think about experience, its arrival into consciousness is already mediated through thought; and thought, even though it may not need a verbal language, is always formulated in symbolic form. The thing itself has to be transformed into something else so that it can be thought about. So we live in a world of approximations on the one hand and constructed meanings on the other.

Problems start if the word and the object are conflated so that the constructed, discursive nature of identity is not acknowledged. This recognition connects the psychological to the philosophical, which is why it seemed important to include a chapter on the philosophical underpinnings of western psychotherapy. If we allow ourselves to think that psychotherapy and counselling emerged in some sort of pure state, uninfluenced by the mood of the times, we are too close to fundamentalist religious doctrine for comfort. All things occur in context.

Although we have concentrated on language, it has been important to include a chapter on the non-verbal therapies. In one way these could have been included as a part of every chapter rather than being confined to one of their own. Obviously the sense of self precedes language, and early communication is entirely non-verbal and extremely effective. Arts therapies range from those that see symbolic expression as sufficient in itself and requiring no translation, to those that use the arts to start a process that will lead eventually to the painting or composition or dance being spoken about and interpreted. Sometimes it is not necessary to explain why you need to hit the drum loudly for ten minutes; but it is necessary to have somebody there witnessing it.

Therapy tries to put into words, or into some form of symbolic and shared expression, that which is as yet unconscious, unarticulated and unthought. One language is simply not enough for this. The multiplicities of approaches, of theories, contribute together to this aim of becoming known in therapy. Through becoming known each has the experience of being a subject, someone who exists not just to their own self but in relation to another. Theories help to name the elusive, the ungraspable, although this must at the same time be acknowledged as beyond naming.

All therapies place great emphasis on the communicated relationship. They do this in different ways, of course. Humanistic therapies emphasize the language of equality, which may include sharing the therapist's own process, occasionally sharing personal information, signalling that the therapist stands alongside and not apart from the client. A psychoanalytic approach is likely to emphasize the use of interpretation, where the therapist offers a possible meaning to the client of their thoughts, feelings or behaviours, using the presenting material and, most importantly, the transference. The humanist might say, 'I feel . . .', the analyst might say, 'You feel . . .'. The words each uses in the consulting room may be very different, and therapists often feel passionately that one or the other way is best. Yet the words themselves are also vehicles for the intent behind them. 'I feel' can be said coldly, critically ('I feel you are holding back in the therapy at the moment'); 'You feel' can be said warmly, inquiringly ('You feel perhaps anxious and a little frightened to let me know any more just at the moment'). Therapy is not about getting the language 'right'. The words matter, but so does the intention behind them.

Gender is one of the clearest demonstrations of the confusion caused by a fundamentalist approach to linguistics. Gender is deeply embedded in language, and language determines our sense of self within a gendered identity. My interest in this area was, if not started then certainly clarified, by some seminars I ran for counselling students in masters training. I asked them to list all the words they could agree as being descriptive of 'masculine' and 'feminine'. Over several groups, it was always impossible to complete this exercise – there was nothing they could agree as an exclusively male or exclusively female characteristic. Yet when asked if they would therefore prefer to agree that there was no essential difference between the genders, this was equally impossible. Difference was believed to exist but it could not be named. The only solution was to proceed as if both of these things were indeed true, and see where that led. The whole concept of difference is oppositional and exclusive, and this is not the lived experience of gender, or in fact of any reality. Masculine may not be the natural derivative of male, nor feminine of female. Linguistic illogicality is not a barrier to descriptive accuracy. What gender illustrates is just how much culture is embedded in language, and how much language defines the limits of a livable, even a thinkable, life.

Language is then an approximation. It allows us to connect with one another through having a common basis for recognition. It reaches broadly over the spoken, written and signed word, over the arts as well as the sciences. It stretches from the detailed definition of a precise moment to the universal sweep of archetypal symbolism. So – what as therapists are we to do with it?

> Each time the analyst speaks, interprets in the analytic situation, he gives something asked of him. What he gives, however, is not a superior answer but a reply. The reply addresses not so much what the patient says (or means), but his call. Being fundamentally a reply to the subject's question, to the force of his address, the interpretive gift is not constative (cognitive) but performative: the gift is not so much a gift of truth, of understanding or of meaning: it is, essentially, a gift of language.
>
> (Felman 1987: 119)

To use language with another is itself a symbolic act; in the therapy room it stands for the desire to meet and to know the client. An authentic response is demonstrated through language and exactness is not required for this intent to be realized. There is no fixed or complete meaning. Much as with this book, the moment that I finish a chapter I think of more that I want to put into it and always of something that I now want to change or take out. The words are the closest I can get to my meaning at the time, and like smoke, they will not last. But they signify a movement towards, a reaching, a shaping. The language itself is the gift.

Nicola Barden

References

Abrams, R. (2006) Lost in translation, *Guardian*, 4 March.

Adams, M.V. (1996) *The Multicultural Imagination: Race, Color and the Unconscious*. London: Routledge.

Adamson, E. (1984) *Art as Healing*. London: Coventure.

Allderidge, P. (1997) *Bethlem Hospital 1247–1997: A Pictorial Record*. Chichester: Phillimore & Co. Ltd.

American Psychiatric Association (APA) (2000) *Diagnostic and Statistical Manual of Mental Disorders* (4th edn). Washington, DC: APA.

Austen, J.L. (1975) *How to Do Things with Words*. Oxford: Clarendon Press.

Bagemihl, B. (1999) *Biological Exuberance: Animal Homosexuality and Natural Diversity*. London: Profile Books.

Bakhtin, M. (1981) Discourse in the novel, in M. Holquist (ed.) *The Dialogic Imagination: Four Essays*. Austin, TX: University of Texas Press.

Bannister, D. and Fransella, F. (1971) *Inquiring Man*. Harmondsworth: Penguin.

Barden, N. (2001) The development of gender identity, in S. Izzard and N. Barden (eds) *Rethinking Gender and Therapy*. Buckingham: Open University Press.

Barnes, G. (2001) Voices of sanity in the conversation of psychotherapy, *Kybernetes*, 30(5/6): 526–50.

Barnes, M. and Berke, J. (1973) *Mary Barnes: Two Accounts of a Journey through Madness*. Harmondsworth: Penguin.

Beard, R.M. (1969) *An Outline of Piaget's Developmental Psychology*. London: Routledge and Kegan Paul.

Bee, H. (1994) *Lifespan Development*. New York: HarperCollins.

Bellaby-Langford, R. (2001) Developmental needs. Paper delivered to MSc in Integrative Psychotherapy, Sherwood Psychotherapy Training Institute/University of Derby, March.

Beck, J.S. (1995) *Cognitive Therapy: Basics and Beyond*. New York: Guildford Press.

Berke, J., Masoliver, C. and Ryan, T.J. (1995) *Sanctuary*. London: Process Press.

Berne, E. (1964) *Games People Play: The Psychology of Human Relationships*. London: Penguin.

Bernstein, B. (1995) Dancing beyond trauma: women survivors of sexual abuse, in F.J. Levy (ed.) *Dance and Other Expressive Art Therapies: When Words Are Not Enough*. London: Routledge.

Bettelheim, B. (1976) *The Uses of Enchantment*. London: Thames and Hudson.

Bickerton, D. (1981) *Roots of Language*. Ann Arbor, MI: Karoma.

Bing, J. and Bergvall, V. (1998) The question of questions: beyond binary thinking, in J. Coates (ed.) *Language and Gender: A Reader*. Oxford: Blackwell.

Bion, W. (1967) *Second Thoughts*. London: Heinemann.

Bodine, A. (1998) Androcentrism in prescriptive grammar: singular 'they', sex-indefinite 'he', and 'he' or 'she', in D. Cameron (ed.) *The Feminist Critique of Language: A Reader* (2nd edn). London: Routledge.

Bollas, C. (1987) *The Shadow of the Object: Psychoanalysis of the Unthought Known*. London: Free Association Books.

Bowlby, J. (1997) *Attachment and Loss* (Vol. 1). London: Pimlico.

Brierly, J. and Barlow, H. (1994) *Give Me a Child Until He Is Seven: Brain Studies and Early Childhood Education*. Falmer: Routledge.

Bristow, J. (1997) *Sexuality*. London: Routledge.

British Deaf Association (1992) *Dictionary of British Sign Language/English*. London: Faber and Faber.

Buber, M. (1958) *I and Thou*. Edinburgh: T&T Clark.

Buber, M. (1967) *A Believing Humanism: My Testament 1902–1965*. London: Humanities Press International.

Bunt, L. (2002a) Suzanna's story: music therapy with a pre-school child, in L. Bunt and S. Hoskyns (eds) *The Handbook of Music Therapy*. Hove: Brunner-Routledge.

Bunt, L. (2002b) Transformation, Ovid and guided imagery and music (GIM), in L. Bunt and S. Hoskyns (eds) *The Handbook of Music Therapy*. Hove: Brunner-Routledge.

Bunt, L. and Hoskyns, S. (2002) Practicalities and basic principles of music therapy, in L. Bunt and S. Hoskyns (eds) *The Handbook of Music Therapy*. Hove: Brunner-Routledge.

Bushnell, I.W.R., Sai, F. and Mullin, J.T. (1989) Neonatal recognition of the mother's face, *British Journal of Developmental Psychology*, 7: 3–15.

Butler, J. (1990) *Gender Trouble: Feminism and the Subversion of Identity*. New York: Routledge.

Butler, J. (1993) *Bodies That Matter: On the Discursive Limits of 'Sex'*. New York: Routledge.

Butterworth, G. and Grover, L. (1988) The origins of referential communication in human infancy, in L. Weisenkrantz (ed.) *Thought Without Language* (A Fyssen Foundation Symposium). Oxford: Oxford University Press.

Camarata, S. and Yoder, P. (2002) Language transactions during development and intervention: theoretical implications for developmental neuroscience, *International Journal of Neuroscience*, 20: 459–65.

Cameron, D. (1998) Introduction, in D. Cameron (ed.) *The Feminist Critique of Language: A Reader* (2nd edn). London: Routledge.

Campbell, J. (1995) *Understanding John Dewey*. Chicago: Open Court.

Carroll, R. (2002) Biodynamic massage in psychotherapy: re-integrating, re-owning and re-associating through the body, in T. Staunton (ed.) *Body Psychotherapy*. Hove: Brunner-Routledge.

Chomsky, N. (1957) *Syntactic Structures*. The Hague: Mouton.

Clarke, I. (2001) Psychosis and spirituality, in S. King-Spooner and C. Newnes (eds) *Spirituality and Psychotherapy*. Ross-on-Wye: PCCS Books.

Clarkson, P. (1991) *Transactional Analysis Psychotherapy: An Integrated Approach*. London: Routledge.

Clarkson, P. (1999) *Gestalt Counselling in Action*. London: Sage Publications.

Clarkson, P. (2001) The transpersonal relationship in counselling, psychology and psychotherapy, in S. King-Spooner and C. Newnes (eds) *Spirituality and Psychotherapy*. Ross-on-Wye: PCCS Books.

Cole, J. (1998) *About Face*. Cambridge, MA: MIT Press.

Cole, P. (1976) Art therapy at the Henderson, *Inscape*, 12.

Constantine, D. (2004) *Collected Poems*. Tarset: Bloodaxe Books.

Darwin, C. ([1859] 1985) *The Origin of Species*. London: Penguin.

Department of Education and Science (DES) (1978) *Special Educational Needs* (The Warnock Report). London: HMSO.

Department of Health (DoH) (2004) *Evidence Based Clinical Practice Guidelines: Treatment Choice in Psychological Therapies and Counselling*. London: HMSO.

Eco, U. (1984) *Semiotics and the Philosophy of Language*. London: Macmillan.

Ehrlich, S. and King, R. (1998) Gender-based language reform and the social construction of meaning, in D. Cameron (ed.) *The Feminist Critique of Language: A Reader* (2nd edn). London: Routledge.

Ellis, A. (1962) *Reason and Emotion in Psychotherapy*. New York: Lyle Stuart.

Evans, D. (ed.) (1968) *Makers of the Twentieth Century: Marx, Nietzsche, Freud*. Upper Saddle River, NJ: Prentice Hall.

Eynon, T. (2001) Metaphor: the impossible translation? *British Journal of Psychotherapy*, 17(31): 353–64.

Feinberg, L. (1996) *Transgender Warriors: Making History from Joan of Arc to Denis Rodman*. Boston: Beacon Press.

Felman, S. (1987) *Jacques Lacan and the Adventure of Insight*. Cambridge, MA: Harvard University Press.

Ferenczi, S. (1953) *The Theory and Technique of Psychoanalysis*. New York: Basic Books.

Forness-Bennett, J. (1997) Credibility, plausibility and autobiographical oral narrative: some suggestions from the analysis of a rape survivor's testimony, in A. Levett, A. Kottler, E. Burman and I. Parker (eds) *Culture, Power and Difference: Discourse Analysis in South Africa*. London and Cape Town: Zed Books and University of Cape Town Press.

Foster, F. (1997) Fear of three dimensionality: clay and plasticine as experimental bodies, in K. Killick and J. Schaverien (eds) *Art, Psychotherapy and Psychosis*. London: Routledge.

Foulkes, S.H. (1964) *Therapeutic Group Analysis*. London: Allen and Unwin.

Freud, S. ([1900a] 1953) The interpretation of dreams, in J. Strachey and A. Freud (eds) *The Standard Edition of the Complete Psychological Works of Sigmund Freud* (Vol. 4). London: Hogarth Press and the Institute of Psycho-Analysis.

Freud, S. ([1900b] 1953) The interpretation of dreams, in J. Strachey and A. Freud (eds) *The Standard Edition of the Complete Psychological Works of Sigmund Freud* (Vol. 5). London: Hogarth Press and the Institute of Psycho-Analysis.

Freud, S. ([1905] 1953) Three essays on the theory of sexuality, in J. Strachey and A. Freud (eds) *The Standard Edition of the Complete Psychological Works of Sigmund Freud* (Vol. 7). London: Hogarth Press and the Institute of Psycho-Analysis.

Freud, S. ([1913] 1995) Totem and taboo, in P. Gay (ed.) *The Freud Reader*. London: Vintage.

Freud, S. ([1915–16] 1963) Introductory lectures on psycho-analysis, in J. Strachey and A. Freud (eds) *The Standard Edition of the Complete Psychological Works of Sigmund Freud* (Vol. 15). London: Hogarth Press and the Institute of Psycho-Analysis.

Freud, S. ([1916] 1963) Symbolism in dreams, in J. Strachey and A. Freud (eds) *The Standard Edition of the Complete Psychological Works of Sigmund Freud* (Vol. 15). London: Hogarth Press and the Institute of Psycho-Analysis.

Freud ([1918] 1995) Wolf Man: history of an infantile neurosis, in P. Gay (ed.) *The Freud Reader*. London: Vintage

Freud, S. ([1923] 1995) The ego and the id, in P. Gay (ed.) *The Freud Reader*. London: Vintage.

Freud, S. ([1925] 1995) An autobiographical study, in P. Gay (ed.) *The Freud Reader*. London: Vintage.

Freud, S. ([1926] 1959) Inhibitions, symptoms and anxiety, in J. Strachey and A. Freud (eds) *The Standard Edition of the Complete Psychological Works of Sigmund Freud* (Vol. 20). London: Hogarth Press and the Institute of Psycho-Analysis.

Freud, S. ([1932] 1990) Femininity, in E. Young-Bruehl (ed.) *Freud on Women*. London: Hogarth Press.

Fried, D.P. (1995) Sue and Jon: working with blind children, in F.J. Levy (ed.) *Dance and Other Expressive Art Therapies: When Words Are Not Enough*. London: Routledge.

Frosh, S. (1994) *Sexual Difference: Masculinity and Psychoanalysis*. London: Routledge.

Frosh, S., Phoenix, A. and Pattman, P. (2002) *Young Masculinities: Understanding Boys in Contemporary Society*. Basingstoke: Palgrave.

Fry, D.B. (1966) The development of the phonological system in the normal and the deaf child, in F. Smith and G.A. Miller (eds) *The Genesis of Language: A Psycholinguistic Approach*. Cambridge, MA: MIT Press.

Furth, H.G. (1966) *Thinking Without Language: Psychological Implications of Deafness*. London: Collier Macmillan.

Gaarder, J. (1968) *Sophie's World*; translator Paulette Moller 1996, London: Phoenix Paperbacks.

Gallop, J. (1984) *Lacan and Literature: A Case for Transference Poetics* 13 301–308.

Garai, J. (2001) Humanistic art therapy, in A.J. Rubin (ed.) *Approaches to Art Therapy: Theory and Technique*. Hove: Brunner-Routledge.

Georgaca, E. (2001) Voices of the self in psychotherapy: a qualitative analysis, *British Journal of Medical Psychology*, 74: 223–36.

Gergen, K. (1990) Therapeutic professions and the diffusion of deficit, *Journal of Mind and Body*, 11: 353–68.

Goffman, I. (1961) *Asylums*. London: Penguin.

Grayling, A.C. (2002) *Russell: A Very Short Introduction*. Oxford: Oxford University Press.

Green, A. ([1979] 2004) Le silence du psychanalyste, *British Journal of Psychotherapy*, 21(2): 229–40.

Gvirtzmann, D. (1990) Bones, self and paradox, Part 1, *Energy and Character*, 21(2): 28–45.

Halberstam, J. (1998) *Female Masculinity*. Durham, NC: Duke University Press.

Hardy, T. ([1874] 1974) *Far From the Madding Crowd*. London: Macmillan.

Harvey, S. (1995) Sandra: the case of an adopted sexually abused child, in F.J. Levy (ed.) *Dance and Other Expressive Art Therapies: When Words Are Not Enough*. London: Routledge.

Heath, G. (2002) Philosophy and psychotherapy: conflict or co-operation? *International Journal of Psychotherapy*, 7(1): 13–52.

Henderson, J.L. (1978) Ancient myths and modern man, in C.G. Jung (ed.) *Man and His Symbols*. London: Picador.

Hillman, J. (1977) An inquiry into image, *Spring: An Annual of Archetypal Psychology and Jungian Thought*, 62–88.

Hinshelwood, R.D. (1991) *A Dictionary of Kleinian Thought*. London: Free Association Books.

Holmes, J. (1998) Women's talk: the question of sociolinguistic universals, in J. Coates (ed.) *Language and Gender: A Reader*. Oxford: Blackwell.

Holmes, J. (2001) *The Search for the Secure Base: Attachment, Psychoanalysis and Narrative*. London: Routledge.

Holmes, J. (2004) The language of psychotherapy: metaphor, ambiguity, wholeness, *British Journal of Psychotherapy*, 21: 209–28.

Holmes, P. (1991) Classical psychodrama: an overview, in P. Holmes and M. Karp (eds) *Psychodrama: Inspiration and Technique*. London: Tavistock/Routledge.

Hycner, R. (1991) *Between Person and Person: Towards a Dialogical Psychotherapy*. Highland, NY: Gestalt Journal Press.

Irigaray, L. ([1977] 1991) The poverty of psychoanalysis, in M. Whitford (ed.) *The Irigaray Reader*. Oxford: Blackwell.

Jacobs, M. (2003) *Sigmund Freud*. London: Sage Publications.

James, W. ([1902] 1961) *The Varieties of Religious Experience*. London: Collier Macmillan.

Janaway, C. (1997) Schopenhauer, in R. Scruton, P. Singer, C. Janaway and M. Tanner (eds) *German Philosophers*. Oxford: Oxford University Press.

Jansons, K.M. (1988) A personal view of dyslexia and of thought without language: discussion, in L. Weiskrantz (ed.) *Thought Without Language* (A Fyssen Foundation Symposium). Oxford: Clarendon Press.

Jennings, S. and Minde, A. (1993) *Art Therapy and Drama Therapy: Masks of the Soul*. London: Jessica Kingsley.

Jones, P. (1996) *Drama as Therapy*. London: Routledge.

Jung, C.G. ([1916] 1976) The transcendent function, in J. Campbell (ed.) *The Portable Jung*. Harmondsworth: Penguin.

Jung, C.G. (1923) *Psychological Types*. London: Kegan Paul, Trench, Trubner & Co. Ltd.

Jung, C.G. ([1931] 1954) The aims of psychotherapy, in H. Read, M. Fordham and G. Adler (eds) *The Collected Works of C.G. Jung* (Vol. 16). London: Routledge and Kegan Paul.

Jung, C.G. (1963) *Memories, Dreams, Reflections*. London: Collins and Routledge and Kegan Paul.

Jung, C.G. (1968) Conscious, unconscious and individuation, in H. Read, M. Fordham and G. Adler (eds) *The Collected Works of C.G. Jung* (Vol. 9). London: Routledge and Kegan Paul.

Jung, C.G. (1976) The difference between eastern and western thinking, in J. Campbell (ed.) *The Portable Jung*. Harmondsworth: Penguin.

Jung, C.G. (1978) Approaching the unconscious, in C.G. Jung (ed.) *Man and His Symbols*. London: Picador.

Kaplan, C. (1998) Language and gender, in D. Cameron (ed.) *The Feminist Critique of Language: A Reader* (2nd edn). London: Routledge.

Kaufmann, G. (1993) *The Psychology of Shame: Theory and Treatment of Shame Based Syndromes*. New York: Springer.

Kennedy, M. (1995) Art-in-therapy: the role of art-communication and picture-art in working with abused deaf clients, in M. Corker (ed.) *Counselling: The Deaf Challenge*. London: Jessica Kingsley.

King-Spooner, S. (2001) The place of spirituality in psychotherapy, in S. King-Spooner and C. Newnes, *Spirituality and Psychotherapy*. Ross-on-Wye: PCCS Books.

Klein, M. ([1930] 1988) The importance of symbol formation in the development of the ego, in M. Klein, *Love, Guilt and Reparation, and Other Works 1921–1945*. London: Virago.

Klein, M. ([1963] 1984) Some reflections on 'The Oresteia', in M. Klein, *Envy and Gratitude and Other Works 1946–1963*. London: Hogarth Press.

Koestler, A. (1979) Introduction, in L.L. Whyte (ed.) *The Unconscious Before Freud*. London: Julian Friedmann.

Kohut, H. (1977) *The Restoration of the Self*. New York: International Universities Press.

Kramer, E. (2001) Sublimation and art therapy, in J.A. Rubin (ed.) *Approaches to Art Therapy: Theory and Technique*. London: Brunner-Routledge.

Kurtz, A. (2004) Introduction, *Journal of Psychology and Psychotherapy: Theory, Research and Practice*, 1(77): 141–4.

Kurtz, R. ([1985] 2002) Hakomi therapy. Self published, in T. Staunton (ed.) *Body Psychotherapy*. Hove: Brunner-Routledge.

Labov, W. (1972) *Sociolinguistic Patterns*. Philadelphia, PA: University of Pennsylvania Press.

Lacan, J. (1979) *The Four Fundamental Concepts of Psychoanalysis*. Harmondsworth: Penguin.

Lachman-Chapin, M. (2001) Self psychology and art therapy, in A.J. Rubin (ed.) *Approaches to Art Therapy: Theory and Technique*. Hove: Brunner-Routledge.

Laing, R.D. (1959) *The Divided Self*. Harmondsworth: Penguin.

Lakoff, G. and Johnson, M. (1980) *Metaphors We Live By*. Chicago: University of Chicago Press.

Lakoff, G. and Johnson, M. (1999) *Philosophy in the Flesh*. New York: Basic Books.

Lakoff, R. (1975) *Language and Women's Place*. New York: Harper and Row.

Lavender, J. and Sobelman, W. (1995) 'I can't have me if I don't have you': working with the borderline personality, in F.J. Levy (ed.) *Dance and Other Expressive Art Therapies: When Words Are Not Enough*. London: Routledge.

Levenson, E.A. (1991) *The Purloined Self: Interpersonal Perspectives in Psychoanalysis*. New York: William Alanson White Institute.

Levy, F.J. (1995a) Introduction, in F.J. Levy (ed.) *Dance and Other Expressive Art Therapies: When Words Are Not Enough*. London: Routledge.

Levy, F.J. (1995b) Nameless: a case of multiplicity, in F.J. Levy (ed.) *Dance and Other Expressive Art Therapies: When Words Are Not Enough*. London: Routledge.

Lichteim, G. (1972) Freud and Marx, in J. Miller (ed.) *Freud: The Man, His World, His Influence*. London: Weidenfield and Nicolson.

Lorber, J. (1994) *Paradoxes of Gender*. New Haven, CT: Yale University Press.

Lowen, A. (1971) *The Language of the Body*. Collier Macmillan.

McDougall, J. (1989) *Theatres of the Body: A Psychoanalytical Approach to Psychosomatic Illness*. London: Free Association Books.

Macey, D. (1988) *Lacan in Contexts*. London: Verso.

McLeod, J. (1997) *Narrative and Psychotherapy*. London: Sage Publications.

McLeod, J. (2003) *An Introduction to Counselling*. Buckingham: Open University Press.

McLynn, F. (1996) *Jung*. London: Bantam Press.

McNeill, D. (1966) Developmental psycholinguistics, in F. Smith and G.A. Miller (eds) *The Genesis of Language: A Psycholinguistic Approach*. Cambridge, MA: MIT Press.

Maslow, A.H. (1987) *Motivation and Personality*. New York: Longman.

Mearns, D. and Thorne, B. (1988) *Person-centred Counselling in Action*. London: Sage Publications.

Mehrabian, A. (1969) *Tactics in Social Influence*. Eaglewood Cliffs, NJ: Prentice Hall.

Mills, S. (1998) The gendered sentence, in D. Cameron (ed.) *The Feminist Critique of Language: A Reader* (2nd edn). London: Routledge.

Mollon, P. (2003) *Releasing the Self: The Healing Legacy of Heinz Kohut*. London: Whurr.

Moreno, J.L. (1946) *Psychodrama I, II and III*. Beacon, NY: Beacon House.

The New English Bible (NEB) (1972) The Bible Societies in association with Oxford University Press and Cambridge University Press.

Nicholson, L. (1994) Interpreting gender, *Signs: Journal of Women in Culture and Society*, 20(1): 79–105.

Orlando-Fantini, P. (2005) Recorded from a discussion in group supervision, November 2005.

Orwell, G. ([1949] 2000) *Nineteen Eighty-Four*. London: Penguin.

Padesky, C.A. (1993) Socratic questioning: changing minds or guiding discovery? Keynote address delivered at the European Congress of Behavioural and Cognitive Therapies, London, 24 September.

Parlett, M. (1993) *British Gestalt Journal*, Oct: 233–44.

Parlett, M. (1993) Towards a More Lewinian Gestalt Therapy, *British Gestalt Journal*, 2: 115–20.

Pedder, J. (1979) Transitional space in psychotherapy and theatre, *British Journal of Medical Psychology*, 52: 37–58.

Peirce, C.S. ([1905] 1974) What pragmatism is, in C. Hartshorne and P. Weiss (eds) *Collected Papers of Charles Sanders Peirce, Vol. V, Pragmatism and Pragmaticism*. Cambridge, MA: The Belknap Press of Harvard University Press.

Perls, F. (1969) *Gestalt Therapy Verbatim*. Lafayette, CA: Real People Press.

Pinker, S. (1994) *The Language Instinct: The New Science of Language and Mind*. London: Penguin.

Pinker, S. (1999) *Words and Rules: The Ingredients of Language*. London: Phoenix.

Pyle, C. (1977) *Lacan's Theory of Language Part 1: 2*. Available at: www.modempool.com/pyle/lacan/1htm (accessed November 2004).

Reich, W. (1927) *The Function of the Orgasm*. New York: Orgone Institute Press.

Reich, W. (1972) *Character Analysis*. New York: Touchstone.

Rogers, C.R. (1951) *Client-centred Therapy: Its Current Practice, Implications and Theory*. London: Constable.

Rogers, N. (2001) Person-centred expressive arts therapy, in J.A. Rubin (ed.) *Approaches to Art Therapy: Theory and Technique*. Hove: Brunner-Routledge.

Ronnberg, J., Soderfeldt, B. and Risberg, J. (2002) The cognitive neuroscience of sign language, *Science Direct*, 105: 237–54.

Rorty, R. (1991) *Philosophical Papers*. Cambridge: Cambridge University Press.

Rosal, M. (2001) Cognitive-behavioural art therapy, in A.J. Rubin (ed.) *Approaches to Art Therapy: Theory and Technique*. Hove: Brunner-Routledge.

Rose, S. (1995) Movement as metaphor: treating chemical addiction, in F.J. Levy (ed.) *Dance and Other Expressive Art Therapies: When Words Are Not Enough*. London: Routledge.

Roth, E. (2001) Behavioural art therapy, in A.J. Rubin (ed.) *Approaches to Art Therapy: Theory and Technique*. Hove: Brunner-Routledge.

Rothschild, B. (2002) Body psychotherapy without touch: applications for trauma therapy, in T. Staunton (ed.) *Body Psychotherapy*. Hove: Brunner-Routledge.

Rubin, G. (1993) Thinking sex: notes for a radical theory of the politics of sexuality, in H. Abelove, A.B. Barale and D.M. Halpern (eds) *The Lesbian and Gay Studies Reader*. New York: Routledge.

Russell R.L. (1989) Language and psychotherapy, *Clinical Psychology Review*, 19: 505–19.

Rutherford, J. (1992) *Men's Silences: Predicaments in Masculinity*. London: Routledge.

Rycroft, C. (1985) *Psychoanalysis and Beyond*. London: Chatto and Windus.

Sabbadini, A. (2004) Listening to silence, *British Journal of Psychotherapy*, 21(2): 229–40.

Sachs, O. (1985) *The Man Who Mistook His Wife for a Hat*. London: Picador.

Samuels, A., Shorter, B. and Plaut, F. (1986) *A Critical Dictionary of Jungian Analysis*. London: Routledge and Kegan Paul.

Saussure, F. de ([1916] 1959) *Course in General Linguistics*. New York: McGraw-Hill.

Schaverien, J. (1987) The scapegoat as talisman: transference in art therapy, in T. Dalley et al. (eds) *Images of Art Therapy: New Developments in Theory and Practice*. London: Tavistock/Routledge.

Schaverien, J. (1997) Transference and transactional objects in the treatment of psychosis, in K. Killick and J. Schaverien (eds) *Art, Psychotherapy and Psychosis*. London: Routledge.

Schaverien, J. (2001) Commentary, in A.J. Rubin (ed.) *Approaches to Art Therapy: Theory and Technique*. Hove: Brunner-Routledge.

Schore, A. (1994) *Affect Regulation and the Origin of the Self: Neurobiology of Emotional Development*. Mahwah, NJ: Erlbaum.

Schore, A. (2001) Effects of a secure attachment relationship on right brain development, affect regulation and infant mental health, *Infant Mental Health*, 22(1–2): 201–69.

Scruton, R. (1997) Kant, in R. Scruton, P. Singer, C. Janaway and M. Tanner (eds) *German Philosophers*. Oxford: Oxford University Press.

Scruton, R. (2002) *Spinoza: A Very Short Introduction*. Oxford: Oxford University Press.

Segal, H. (1986) *The Work of Hanna Segal: A Kleinian Approach to Clinical Practice*. London: Free Association Books.

Segal, J. (1992) *Melanie Klein*. London: Sage Publications.

Singer, P. (1997) Hegel, in R. Scruton, P. Singer, C. Janaway and M. Tanner (eds) *German Philosophers*. Oxford: Oxford University Press.

Singer, P. (2001) *Hegel: A Very Short Introduction*. Oxford: Oxford University Press.

Skailes, C. (1997) The forgotten people, in K. Killick and J. Schaverien (eds) *Art, Psychotherapy and Psychosis*. London: Routledge.

Skinner, B.F. (1957) *Verbal Behaviour*. New York: Appleton-Century-Crofts.

Slobin, D. (1971) *Psycholinguistics*. Glenview, IL: Scott, Foresman and Company.

Sloboda, A. and Bolton, R. (2002) Music therapy in forensic psychiatry: a case study with musical commentary, in L. Bunt and S. Hoskyns (eds) *The Hand-book of Music Therapy*. Hove: Brunner-Routledge.

Soler, C. (2000) The curse on sex, in R. Saleci (ed.) *Sexuation*. Durham, NC: Duke University Press.

Somerville, S.B. (2000) *Queering the Color Line: Race and the Invention of Homosexuality in American Culture*. Durham, NC: Duke University Press.

Sontag, S. (1991) *Illness as Metaphor and Aids and Its Metaphors*. London: Penguin.

Spender. D. (1998) Extracts from 'Man Made Language', in D. Cameron (ed.) *The Feminist Critique of Language: A Reader* (2nd edn). London: Routledge.

Stapledon, O. (1939) *Philosophy and Living* (Vol. 1). Harmondsworth: Penguin.

Staunton, T. (2002) Sexuality and body psychotherapy, in T. Staunton (ed.) *Body Psychotherapy*. Hove: Brunner-Routledge.

Stern, D. (2000) *The Interpersonal World of the Infant: A View from Psychoanalysis and Development Psychology*. London: Basic Books.

Stevens, R. (1983) *Freud and Psychoanalysis*. Buckingham: Open University Press.

Stokoe, W.C. (1960) *Sign Language Structure: An Outline of the Visual Communication Systems of the American Deaf*. Occasional Paper 8. University of Buffalo, USA.

Tannen, D. (1992) *You Just Don't Understand: Women and Men in Conversation*. London: Virago.

Tanner, M. (1997) Nietzsche, in R. Scruton, P. Singer, C. Janaway and M. Tanner (eds) *German Philosophers*. Oxford: Oxford University Press.

Tompkins, P. and Lawley, J. (1997) Less is more . . . the art of clean language, *Rapport Magazine*, 35. Available at: www. cleanlanguage.co.uk.

Tompkins, P., Sullivan, W. and Lawley, J. (2005) Tangled spaghetti in my head, *Therapy Today*, 16(8): 32–6.

Totton, N. (2002a) Foreign bodies: recovering the history of body psycho-therapy, in T. Staunton (ed.) *Body Psychotherapy*. Hove: Brunner-Routledge.

Totton, N. (2002b) The future for body psychotherapy, in T. Staunton (ed.) *Body Psychotherapy*. Hove: Brunner-Routledge.

Totton, N. (2004) Two ways of being helpful, *Counselling and Psychotherapy Journal*, 15(10): 5–8.

Trask, R.L. and Mayblin, B. (2000) *Introducing Linguistics*. Cambridge: Icon Books.

Troemel-Ploetz, S. (1998) Selling the apolitical, in J. Coates (ed.) *Language and Gender: A Reader*. Oxford: Blackwell.

Vas Dias, S. (2001) When do I know I'm a girl? The development of a sense of self as female in the early infant, in S. Izzard and N. Barden (eds) *Rethinking Gender and Therapy*. Buckingham: Open University Press.

von Franz, M.L. (1970) *The Interpretation of Fairytales*. London: Spring.

von Franz, M.L. (1978) The process of individuation, in C.G. Jung (ed.) *Man and His Symbols*. London: Picador.

Waller, D. (1991) *Becoming a Profession: The History of Art Therapy in Britain 1940–1982*. London: Routledge.

Wampold, B.E. (2001) *The Great Psychotherapy Debate*. Mahwah, NJ: Erlbaum.

Weininger, O. (1992) *Melanie Klein: From Theory to Reality*. London: Karnac.

Wells, A. (1997) *Cognitive Therapy of Anxiety Disorders: A Practice Manual and Conceptual Guide*. Chichester: John Wiley and Sons.

West, C. and Fenstermaker, S. (1995) Doing difference, *Gender and Society*, 9(1): 8–37.

White, M. and Epson, D. (1990) *Narrative Means to Therapeutic Ends*. New York: Norton.

Whitford, M. (1991) *Luce Irigaray: Philosophy in the Feminine*. London: Routledge.

Whitmont, E.C. (1978) *The Symbolic Quest: Basic Concepts of Analytical Psychology*. Princeton, NJ: Princeton University Press.

Whyte, L.L. (1979) *The Unconscious Before Freud*. London: Julian Friedmann.

Wilchins, R. (2004) *Queer Theory, Gender Theory*. Los Angeles: Alyson Publications.

Wilson, L. (2001) Symbolism and art therapy, in A.J. Rubin (ed.) *Approaches to Art Therapy: Theory and Technique*. Hove: Brunner-Routledge.

Winnicott, D.W. ([1951] 1992) Transitional objects and transitional phenomena, in D.W. Winnicott, *Through Paediatrics to Psychoanalysis: Collected Papers*. London: Karnac Books and the Institute of Psycho-Analysis.

Winnicott, D.W. ([1954] 1992) The depressive position in normal emotional development, in D.W. Winnicott, *Through Paediatrics to Psychoanalysis: Collected Papers*. London: Karnac Books and the Institute of Psycho-Analysis.

Winnicott, D.W. ([1958] 1990) The capacity to be alone, in D.W. Winnicott, *The Maturational Processes and the Facilitating Environment*. London: Karnac Books and the Institute of Psycho-Analysis.

Winnicott, D.W. ([1960a] 1990) The theory of the parent–infant relationship, in D.W. Winnicott *The Maturational Processes and the Facilitating Environment*. London: Karnac Books and the Institute of Psycho-Analysis.

Winnicott, D.W. ([1960b] 1990) String: a technique of communication, in D.W. Winnicott *The Maturational Processes and the Facilitating Environment*. London: Karnac Books and the Institute of Psycho-Analysis.

Winnicott, D.W. ([1963] 1990) The development of the capacity for concern, in D.W. Winnicott, *The Maturational Processes and the Facilitating Environment*. London: Karnac Books and the Institute of Psycho-Analysis.

Winnicott, D.W. (1991) *Playing and Reality*. London: Tavistock/Routledge.

Wittgenstein, L. ([1922] 1963) *Tractatus Logico-Philosophicus*. London: Routledge and Kegan Paul.

Wittgenstein, L. (1958) *Philosophical Investigations*. Oxford: Blackwell.

Wood, C. (1997) The history of art therapy and psychosis (1938–95), in K. Killick and J. Schaverien (eds) *Art, Psychotherapy and Psychosis*. London: Routledge.

World Health Organization (WHO) (2003) *International Classification of Diseases (ICD 10)*. Geneva: WHO.

Wright, J.K. (2004) The passion of science, the precision of poetry: therapeutic writing – a review of the literature, in G. Bolton, S. Howlett, C. Lago and J.K. Wright (eds) *Writing Cures: An Introductory Handbook of Writing in Counselling and Psychotherapy*. Hove: Brunner-Routledge.

Wright, N. (2006) recorded from part of collegiate discussion at Sherwood Psychotherapy Training Institute.

Yon, K. (1993) Expanding human potential through music, in B. Warren (ed.) *Using the Creative Arts in Therapy: A Practical Introduction*. London: Routledge.

Young, I.M. (2005) *Female Body Experience: 'Throwing Like a Girl' and Other Essays*. Oxford: Oxford University Press.

Index

Mind
  see also Brain
  Cartesian, 23, 24
  Greek philosophy, 23
  individuals, 27
  mind/body dualism, 25, 28, 68
  universality, 27
Mollon, P., 20, 55, 82, 83, 86, 89
Moreno, J.L., 72
Music therapy, 77–9

Narrative therapies, 51–2
Neuroscience, 15–17, 20
Nicholson, L., 107
Nietzsche, Friedrich Wilhelm, 26, 28, 29
North America
  indigenous people, 33
  pragmatism, 32–3
  psychotherapy, 33
  zeitgeist, 31

Object-relations school, 27, 43, 51
Oedipus complex, 40, 52, 98
Orlando-Fantini, P., 92
Orwell, George, 34
Otherness, 17–18, 71, 76, 81–93
Out-of-sight object, 44, 66

Padesky, C.A., 57
Palov, Ivan Petrovich, 10
Panini, 9
Parlett, M., 54
Pascal, Blaise, 25
Pedder, J., 91
Perls, F., 33, 54
Person-centred approach, 55
Personal construct system, 86–7
Philosophy
  generic themes, 29–33
  Greek philosophy, 23
  ontological background, 21–36
  unconscious, 21, 23, 24, 28
Piaget, Jean, 10, 13, 66
Pidgin, 11
Pierce, C.S., 32

Pinker, S., 9, 10, 11, 12, 13, 14, 15, 34–5
Plato, 23, 28
Post-modernism, 22, 51, 105
Pragmatism, 32–3
Primitive languages, 8
Process, 69–70
Projection, 53
Prologue, 1
Proto-Indo-European (PIE), 9
Psycho-educational approaches, 63
Psychodynamic therapy, 51, 87
Psychotherapy
  see also Therapies
  differing approaches vii-viii
  dominant language, 89
  geography, viii
  intentional relationship, 87
  medium of language, 7
  North America, 33
  rapprochement, viii
Pyle, C., 93

Rationalism, 22, 24–5, 51
Reich, W., 67, 68
Religion
  Christianity, 23, 29, 45, 47, 48
  cross symbolism, 45, 47
  Freud (Sigmund), 30
  Jung (Carl Gustav), 45, 46–7
  spirit influence, 23
Repression, 37–8, 67–8
Retroflection, 53–4
Rogers, Carl Ransom, 33, 52
Rogers, N., 62
Roosevelt, Franklin Delano, 32
Rorty, Richard McKay, 33
Rosal, M., 63
Rose, S., 71
Roth, E., 63
Rothschild, B., 69
Royal Bethlehem Hospital, 72
Rubin, G., 100
Russell, Bertrand, 32
Russell, R.L., 52, 93
Rutherford, J., 95